SARAH E. BROWN

POWER TO THE STARTUP PEOPLE

HOW TO GROW YOUR STARTUP CAREER
WHEN YOU'RE NOT THE FOUNDER

HybridGlobal
PUBLISHING

Published by
Hybrid Global Publishing
301 E 57th Street, 4th fl
New York, NY 10022

Manufactured in the United States of America, or in the United Kingdom when distributed elsewhere.

Brown, Sarah E.
    Power to the Startup People: How To Grow Your Startup Career When You're Not The Founder
    LCCN: 2018957515
    ISBN: 978-1-948181-25-9
    eBook: 978-1-948181-26-6

Cover design: Emma Hall at The Frontispiece
Copyediting: Claudia Volkman
Interior design: Claudia Volkman
Photo credits: Deirdre Blatt

www.sarahbrownmarketing.com

TABLE OF CONTENTS

INTRODUCTION

I'm lounging in the living room of a vacation home located in the high country of Colorado with a handful of close friends from Boulder. We each work for startups of various sizes and maturity. We've rented the home for the weekend to relax in the nearby hot springs and hike local mountain trails, as well as set aside time from our harried schedules to discuss our hopes, dreams—and startup careers. As the sun sets and the dry mountain air cools, we bundle up with blankets and take turns sharing life updates, which, especially this particular weekend, offer a snapshot into the variety and complexity of startup life:[1]

- Devon, a software engineer for a small Denver-based tech startup, has just returned to Colorado after a few weeks spent learning a new form of meditation in Amsterdam, where he worked remotely for his startup full-time the entire trip.

- Warren, also an engineer, is in the process of moving from Boulder to Boston to accompany his partner, Kat, who will be doing graduate work there. While in Boston, he will work remotely for his SF- and Boulder-based employer. He wonders whether a promotion is possible when he leaves his home office in Boulder, and whether working remotely will hinder—or help—his chances of being promoted to engineering manager.

- Kat, Warren's partner, used to run the marketing for a popular lifestyle ecommerce brand, and is now a project manager for a national meal delivery company that has just acquired her local Boulder-based meal delivery startup. Kat is trying to figure out how to stay sane during the acquisition and negotiate a comp package that will make her transition to graduate school as low-stress and lucrative as possible.

- Jenny, who holds business and law degrees, works at a well-known tech startup accelerator where she coaches startup teams all day. She is at the director level currently and yearns to be on the executive team with a real say in decision-making at the highest levels. She is considering whether she can make this happen in her current role or if she should join a startup—or perhaps even a Venture Capital (VC) firm.

- Matt, a serial entrepreneur, did a stint as an employee at his own company before realizing he missed the control of being first in command. After recently buying out his business partner, he is navigating the transition back to being the CEO.

Then there's me: currently between jobs, having just left my remote position as Marketing Director at a Palo Alto-based tech company with offices worldwide and in the process of moving back to Silicon Valley to join an SF-based company to build and run their content marketing team.

This is startup life. There are countless opportunities and choices, flexibility is high, and change is the only constant. My friends and I have mentors and decades of experience among us. We have read books written for startup founders, taken courses at business schools (and even taught them), and many of us mentor other companies and startup employees. But when it comes down to making day-to-day decisions about negotiations, where to work, when to leave, and how to do our best work, sometimes it can feel as though, no matter how much experience we have, to some degree we are all shooting from the hip.

In today's tech startup world, career paths are nonlinear. Startup founders can be worth millions before their mid-twenties. On the flip side, some of us invest our best working years at startups that suddenly shut down. By some estimates, nearly 90 percent of startups end in failure.[2] A startup career can be rewarding, but it often can be challenging and confusing.

Startup careers are a relatively new concept. In *The Startup of You*, authors Reid Hoffman and Ben Casnocha describe the past job market as an "escalator." If you put your head down and worked your way up the corporate hierarchy, you could enjoy the fruits of success: a company-sponsored pension and government-sponsored Social Security. Hoffman and Casnocha explain that this "escalator" is now "jammed at every level."[3]

This is especially true at startups, where we employees forge our own career paths. Indeed, few of our career trajectories are alike, and there is little in the way of advice directly aimed at us. Most literature is written for the purpose of helping founders become better at their craft, or helping employees become founders. The consensus within the industry appears to be that a successful startup career culminates in founding your own company. Yet many of us are fulfilled as employees. We want to contribute, but many of us don't want to run companies. We want to know how to have outstanding careers as the people charged with growing tech companies from all levels of the organization.

Employees are immensely powerful and essential to the success of startups. As the makers and sellers of the software and products that are forging our future, we have the power to shape the industry. Techstars, a top accelerator for startups, calls hiring the right employees "the single most important founder skill."[4]

While a ton of proverbial ink has been spilled on how to "crush it" as a founder or startup leader, there's very little in the way of guidance for how employees can hack our own careers. If we're lucky, we find mentors who have had careers we admire. But we may never find these people. Or, if we do, it may be too late, or their expertise in the particular area with which we need help may be limited.

If you're reading this, you may already have a successful tech startup career and want to know how to take it to the next level. Or you may be looking for your first startup job out of college or high school, or perhaps you have a corporate job and would like to know what it's like to transition into a startup. This book offers advice about getting what you need (or giving what others need) in a startup, whether you're already working in one or think you want to.

Entrepreneurs get the lion's share of glory, but much of the work is done by us: the contributors, the team. It takes a special set of skills to do well in this environment, and I've become obsessed with learning how to succeed so I can excel in my own career and help others succeed too. At the time of publishing, I am a Director of Content Marketing at a fast-growing venture-funded tech startup based in the San Francisco Bay Area. I earn a salary that I never would have imagined growing up in a family of academics. I have worked for tech startups with presences in multiple countries and cities, at many stages of funding. For a half-decade, I ran a successful startup marketing consulting business for software-as-a-service (SaaS) companies. I have worked as a freelancer and contract worker, as a full-time employee, as an individual contributor, and as a team leader. I have lived through startup acquisitions and startup failures and have spent nearly a decade learning on the job and from mentors, coaches, and courses.

This book was born out of my desire to find answers to my own questions about how to have the best startup career possible, while ideally avoiding some pitfalls that, unfortunately, are hard to foresee unless you have a direct mentor relationship with someone who has experienced a similar situation. This book is focused on utility, including how to navigate some predictable, crucial career "nodal moments," such as when and how to ask for a promotion and raise, how to raise a family and grow your career simultaneously, how to navigate all-too-common startup failures as an employee, and what to do if you're working for a company that gets acquired.

After reading this book, you'll know the answers to the following questions:

- How will I know if I should try working at a startup?
- How will I know if the startup I've chosen is the "right" one?
- How much does my title matter?
- How do I balance startup life with "life" life?
- At what point should I ask for a promotion, and if I don't receive it, when should I move on in order to be at a higher status and stay competitive in my field?

I am not the be-all and end-all startup career expert. Far from it. I am like you, a startup employee (or future startup employee) who wants to navigate my career as successfully as possible, while enjoying the journey along the way. While this book is not by any means exhaustive, it will hopefully help you make more sense of the world of tech startups and make better decisions about your career along the way.

I have a greater purpose for sharing this information. I truly believe that we, the startup people, hold the power of the tech industry in our hands. By taking command of our own startup careers, we will make a greater impact at the companies that are shaping our future. As the world grapples with questions about the nature of technology in our lives, with concerns about privacy and data and our looming automated economy, we, the employees who make this ecosystem work, will have to decide which companies deserve our time, sweat, and tears. My goal for publishing this book is to give us more choices and more power to shape our own destiny, so that we can in turn enrich the tech ecosystem with our talents. **Power to the startup people!**

PART ONE

FINDING YOUR STARTUP

Tech startups are as unique and varied as the people within them. Whether you're already working at a startup or considering the move to one, the sections in this chapter can help you find the best fit.

ONE

WHAT IT'S LIKE TO BE A STARTUP EMPLOYEE

Why would anyone want to work for a startup? If you're thinking of joining a startup, this chapter highlights how working for startups is different from working at larger, mature companies, and why you might or might not want to join one.

Why It's Not Like Working at an Established Company

Startup life as parodied on the HBO show *Silicon Valley* is a surprisingly accurate (if hyperbolized, to be sure) reflection of what it's like to work within the tech industry. We have nap pods and coconut water, and sometimes we stay up all night coding. But the parody can't convey what it's really like to work at a startup. If you're considering joining one, especially if you currently work at a bigger company, some differences will be apparent right away.

According to serial entrepreneur and investor Jenny Lefcourt in her blog post "Beware of the Beautiful Resume," there's a difference between "big-company" employees and startup employees. She says:

Big-company people care a lot about their relative status and security. Having power within the organization is key to their comfort. They focus on things like titles, the budget they control, and how many people report to them. This type of person wants to feel confident that they are better than their peers. They don't like to make mistakes, especially if the mistakes are visible to others.[5]

Not all "big-company" people identify with Lefcourt's description, and many of them eventually join startups—and enjoy it. Rather than label yourself a startup person or a big company person, it's more helpful to focus on your current career goals. Think about whether you're interested in working in a less stable, more high-risk environment or a bigger company where growth may be slower and risk lower.

Startup people are special. When working for a company we believe in, we can bring an incredible amount of passion, energy, and dedication to our work. The desire to work within an area that ignites one's passion while directly impacting business outcomes inspires many to make the transition.

Many of us have had negative experiences at larger companies, which compels us to found or join startups. Startup leader and former CEO Matt Harada joined a big firm after college, and his experience there drove him to make the switch to startups.

I was in a boring role where I saw middle-aged overweight men working in windowless cubicles. . . . They'd leave on the dot at 5:00 p.m. I didn't want to work in a big company where people didn't care about work. Startups are resource-constrained, but they are often able to provide excitement, learning opportunities and equity, which may become valuable.

So how do you make the switch from a bigger company to a startup? While we'll dive directly into the ins and outs of finding startup jobs and offer negotiation tips later in the book, the first step is to recognize that you really can do it. There will be barriers, but others have overcome them—and you can, too.

Ad technology company Sovrn's Chief of Staff Sarah Innocenzi is often approached by people from larger, more corporate companies inquiring about tech startup opportunities. Innocenzi made the transition from the corporate to the startup world and has noticed some bias toward those shifting from big companies to startups.

"There is a stereotype associated with being from a larger company: that you're not going to understand how to be nimble and comfortable with ambiguity," says Innocenzi. "I work harder now than I did when I was layered within a larger company, but where I'm investing my time, I can actually feel and see the impact I'm making. If that appeals to you, you can overcome the stereotypes and make the transition successfully."

Making the Transition: You Can Do It!
In summary, it is common for people joining startups from corporate environments to worry about the transition. If you are willing to learn and grow, don't worry too much about your skills; likely the abilities you've honed elsewhere will translate to startup life. The bottom line: be confident in

what you know, and humble enough to be willing to learn. If you want to work at a startup, go for it!

Reasons to Work at a Startup
Opportunities to Earn a Good Living
If you're in the startup world for the money, a quick disclaimer: depending on your skill set and whether you have an advanced degree, you could probably earn more at a larger company sooner. That being said, you can earn six figures at a startup within several years, even without any post-secondary education.

Many who work for startups do hold advanced degrees, but these are not a requirement for all roles. This point comes with the major caveat that startups often do not offer the same level of cash compensation as large companies, and an equity payout is not guaranteed. However, some tech companies—especially venture-funded ones and more mature startups—offer an opportunity to earn a higher paycheck compared to other industries.

Easier to Make a Visible Impact
At their heart, tech startups build innovative products and services to serve a market need. When people talk about "disruption," they mean that a startup enters a market, usually one that is previously underserved, or serves said market as a more convenient, cheaper alternative to the current options. Entrepreneur Clay Christensen first introduced the concept of disruption as a framework in his book *The Innovator's Dilemma.*[6]

Whether you are a developer coding a new feature that will change how people interact with the world or working in HR to ensure your team is taken care of and able to perform at their best, you will have ample opportunities to contribute to the disruptive technology products and/or services your company delivers and contribute to your company's mission. This is as true for the engineer who writes code for software as it is for the salesperson who sells it. To sweeten the deal, if and when your company exits (usually this means when it is sold), you may get a piece of that success if you negotiate equity.

Lower Barriers to Entry for Your Career

Startups can provide great job opportunities for people with varying levels of experience. Graduating from an institute of higher learning is not a requisite at many tech companies, which may be attractive to you depending on your level of education.

Many startups hire candidates right out of high school or college. Entrepreneur and mentor Hiten Shah says many of his employees never went to college. Hiten says that in a startup, the lack of formal education can even be a boon because of a perception that these people are more likely to have "hustle" and "honed practical skills."

A 2014 report cited in the *New York Times* found that "almost half of the technology jobs in [New York City] are filled by people without college degrees."[7] Unlike startups, most corporate environments place greater emphasis on bachelor's and advanced degrees.

While many formal academic paths are available and may be helpful in advancing your startup career (computer science degrees, finance degrees, business management degrees, MBAs, etc.), they are not necessarily essential to succeeding at a startup. What you *do* need is a willingness to take learning into your own hands and adopt a growth mindset. We'll discuss this later in the chapter on hacking your productivity and doing the best work of your life.

In addition, developer bootcamps enable people lacking previous technical education to switch careers or specialties. As we'll discuss later, though, a technical background isn't required for many roles at startups.

Flexible, Nontraditional Work Environments

Startups are likely to offer benefits such as flexible hours, locations, work-from-home opportunities, and more. When startups grow and become "scale-ups," they often move to bona fide campuses with more amenities, and some even offer private transportation to and from the office.

There are both drawbacks and benefits to these campuses. One engineer who works at Facebook's office in Menlo Park reports that he spends the majority of his time at work because of all of the amenities it offers. Tech companies that can afford it design their campuses to maximize employee time. One Google employee reports that he works with many people with young families who leave early to pick up their kids, so the office is usually quiet after 5:00 p.m. The free food, he says, helps everyone to be more productive and saves time— not just for work, but to go to a fitness class or go home early. From a company perspective, the more convenient your life, the more time you'll have to be productive in all ways.

Many startups can't offer an on-site gym, snack wall, or nap pod, but they may make up for this in other ways, perhaps offering flexible hours or the option to work from home.

It is important not to generalize, though; some smaller start-ups do not offer many perks and don't embrace a flexible work culture, and some larger companies don't offer tons of campus amenities. Many companies of all sizes foster cultures where staying at work all the time isn't expected.

Personal Growth and Learning

Startups can provide ample learning opportunities. While working at one, you will get the opportunity to wear many hats and learn along the way. If you are up for the challenge, many startups will give you the chance to try different things and learn new skills and technologies.

"It's the people who understand learning comes from being uncomfortable that belong in a startup," says Sovrn's Sarah Innocenzi.

"It is constantly challenging you. Every time I get over a hump, there is another hump. You have to be OK with that to make the transition to a startup. It's a never-ending upward hill. Even when you reach the top, there's another hill for you to climb."

Downsides of Working at a Startup

Startup life can be intense. You won't always be doing the things that excite you most, and the experience will most often not be glamorous. The pace, chaos, and stress of startups also can take a toll. Here are a few of the main drawbacks to startup life.

It Isn't Sexy

MergeLane Co-founder Sue Heilbronner likes to emphasize to her portfolio companies how "unsexy" startup life is.

There isn't enough staff. Someone has to clean out the fridge. You need to have a schedule for cleaning out the fridge. Someone has to deal with payroll. Even if you use a modern payroll service that's SaaS-based, it's still a pain to do payroll. You sometimes earn less money (often). At most startups you won't get a full benefits package, like a matching 401k.

Are you willing to put in the elbow grease and have an "everyone pitches in" mentality?

Volatility

Startup volatility can be nerve-racking, not only for the founders who take on risk, but for employees who stake their livelihoods on an emerging company. Startups may not be stable employment options, especially in their earlier stages. A change in cash flow or funding can lead to rapid changes in startup employees' lives.

Take note: if you're used to working at a large company that offers many benefits, can you live without some or all of them? Would it negatively impact you or your family to give up stability?

Ambiguity

Becoming comfortable with ambiguity has opened many doors for me and many others in our startup careers. But startup ambiguity can also be very challenging. Startup employment can involve constantly switching directions, making decisions with little information, and in general trying to make sense of confusion on a daily basis.

Venture capitalist, Techstars founder, and prolific author of startup books and blogs Brad Feld says the people most likely to thrive at a startup are those who can adapt to frequent change and deliver value in ambiguous circumstances.

"Startups are a mess," says Feld. "They are extremely chaotic, and things change constantly. There are a lot of parts of the startup experience that are exciting, but many aspects are very ambiguous, stressful, and frustrating."

Feld says that it's important to ask yourself whether you are truly interested in and aligned with the work and founding team.

"Is the company doing something that you're interested in? Joining a startup for something you're not into makes it harder," says Feld. "You're going to constantly be in this environment where things don't work, don't make sense, and you experience severe ups and downs and inconsistency."

Dave Cass, an entrepreneur who teaches entrepreneurship at Leeds School of Business, University of Colorado Boulder, says top traits for startup employees include the ability to constantly operate outside your comfort zone and become adept at providing value in ambiguous circumstances. Cass teaches his business school students to develop resilience around the unknown. For example, he never provides an exact course schedule on his syllabus. When students inquire about this, he explains that rigid planning structure isn't how the startup world works and that, like a startup, he will be listening to feedback and adjusting the class based on the goals of the course and the needs of the learners.

"Nowhere in life will the next four months be precisely scheduled for you, nor will it ever go according to plan.

Circumstances will always change in that time period," Cass tells his students at the beginning of the semester. "Becoming comfortable with a level of ambiguity will help build the crucial skills of flexibility, adaptability, and proactive planning."

No Place to Hide

Entrepreneurs Steli Efti and Hiten Shah argue that personal attributes that aren't congruent with startup life include a need for rigidity, predictability, and structure and a strong affinity for titles.

Shah says, "You can't hide in a startup." He explains that in larger companies, people can "hide in the corner," doing only passable work.

"In a startup if you do mediocre work, it's obvious," says Shah. "People who are satisfied with coasting should consider working elsewhere."[8]

Burnout and the Toll on Mental Health

Considering the ambiguity, high pressure, and stressful environments of the startup world, it's not surprising that mental health issues are rampant in tech communities. New studies and research are coming out around the incidences of depression, anxiety, and other mental health issues in the startup community.

In *Killing It*, REBBL CEO and former executive at Clif Bar Sheryl O'Laughlin writes about her own struggle with mental health issues while running a company. She says this isn't unique to her experience: "If you listen closely in Silicon Valley, you can start to hear new murmurings about failure, depression, and the growing problem of drug abuse among the valley's most intense."[9]

But it isn't just founders who are struggling; while they may be closest to the pressure, no one is immune from the intense startup life, no matter what their role. On a positive note, attention around mental health in the startup community is increasing, including an awareness that it's not just founders or CEOs who are afflicted.

VC Brad Feld and others write about how the stigma surrounding mental health can prevent startup workers from admitting their depression or other mental health issues and getting the help they need.[10] Having conversations about real ways to shift unhealthy startup cultures is a great step forward. Some startups now even "pitch mental wellness as a perk."[11]

Personal Relationships Can Suffer

Working for a startup can be all-encompassing; finding time for your family and important relationships can be a challenge. VC Brad Feld wrote *Startup Life* with his wife, Amy Batchelor, in which they describe how they navigate these issues. They advise discussing your career goals with those closest to you, thinking about how you'd like your startup life and your intimate life to relate, and establishing boundaries to enjoy both. This may mean working as a family to determine times when you'll be offline, and choosing not to work for a company that won't respect your weekends or PTO.

Final Thoughts

The downsides to startups are real. It takes a strong commitment to avoid burnout and ensure that you're able to live the life you want while working hard. There is no shame in getting help if you're struggling, or leaving startups if you find the whole industry not suitable to your lifestyle. Everyone has to decide for themselves.

CHAPTER TWO

UNDERSTANDING YOUR STARTUP

Your experience working for a startup will vary depending on company size, mission, location, values, market segment, and more. Startup investor Semil Shah, quoted in the *New York Times,* highlights the confusion around the terminology, since the term *startup* encapsulates a wide range of company types:

> People don't realize the word startup is a broad concept that includes everything from a proven entrepreneur raising $15 million to a guy with money from friends and family. To an outsider . . . "they're both the same."[12]

Technology has made it easier and cheaper than ever to create software, which means there are more companies being created and, as a result, more competition.[13] Each year, hundreds of thousands of startups are founded—the majority of which will fail within the first year.

According to Deborah Gage in "The Venture Capital Secret: 3 out of 4 Start-Ups Fail," more than 90 percent of startups go bust.[14] You might join a company whose massive success will turn you into a millionaire, but more likely, you'll work for a startup that fails, or perhaps one that's by many measures successful but never reaches the famed "unicorn" status (defined as surpassing $1B valuation).[15]

It could be possible to bet correctly on the next hyper-successful company, but it is unlikely. Instead, Hiten Shah suggests trying to find a company whose mission aligns with your own and whose team, product, and role match your personal values and goals. Most importantly, he says, is choosing a company where you can learn and make an impact. If you work for a startup that fails, which is likely, you will at least have grown in the process and will have become much more ready for your next move.

In this chapter, we'll discuss a few of the startup differentiators that can make an impact on your experience.

Startup Sizes

As startups grow, they build more organizational structure. A more mature startup may offer more formal growth paths, better compensation and benefits, and more stability overall. Earlier-stage startups lack processes but can offer more opportunities to wear many hats and contribute across the organization. In *Entering StartUpLand,* venture capitalist and startup veteran Jeffrey Bussgang provides a useful discussion on how startups differ based on a number of employees.

Bussgang outlines these stages:

- "Jungle"—pre-product/market fit (around 1-50 employees)
- "Dirt Road"—post-product/market fit, pre-scaling sales and marketing (around 50–250 employees)

- "Highway"—post-scaling sales and
  marketing (around 250-5k employees)[16]

In a big organization, there are usually more than enough people and clear structures in place for getting work done. On the other hand, startup employees require a high degree of self-direction.

"If you're at a startup that's smaller, be hyper self-directed, because people don't have the time or energy to tell you details," Hiten Shah advises.

This doesn't mean that others at startups don't want to or can't help you; it's likely that they are overloaded themselves. At larger startups, there is training in place to make this easier, whereas a lot of young startups don't have things like formal employee onboarding. This puts team members who aren't naturally self-directed at a disadvantage.

Once startups grow to a certain size—sometimes referred to as "scale-ups"—significant changes occur. We'll talk more about this later in the book, but for now, understand that once a startup hits a critical mass, it is no longer going to behave like a startup, and many of these insights don't apply.

Things Change When a Company Scales
Early employees may notice that many things feel, look, and operate differently as the company grows. Often, early employees get more management above them as a company matures, which for some may be frustrating if they had experienced a high degree of autonomy previously.

"It can be hard for early employees," says Yoav Lurie, Founder and CEO of SimpleEnergy. "In many cases, early employees have a special role and bring historical knowledge and insight and background about the founding and origin story, but they may feel over time like the company has outgrown them."

Early employees' roles and activities may evolve, and their work environment often changes from sitting next to the founder and CEO to being in a delineated department on a different floor. Even though many of these changes are "practical," it can be hard for people to accept them if they are used to a high degree of autonomy and connection to leadership.

Funding Status

Funding status changes how your startup operates. A startup that is self-funded operates differently from one that is not.

Differences in Employee Experience at Funded versus Self-Funded Companies

Many companies raise money from investors for building, marketing, and selling products. Sources of outside investment may include:

- Private equity

- Bank loans

- Startup accelerators such as Y Combinator and Techstars that provide seed funding in exchange for equity in a company

- Angel investors who invest their own money

- Venture capitalists (VCs), who invest other people's money (these people are called limited partners (LPs)

Many startups, over their lifecycle, receive funding from some combination of the above. If you work for a self-funded company, this money is raised from customer revenue. This means that self-funded companies have to be profitable, and they are usually unable to grow as quickly as other companies. Often (but not always) they can't afford to pay as well in early stages.

At self-funded companies, profit is one of the most important metrics, especially early on. At funded companies, external investors often value growth over profit. Growth can come in the form of revenue, users, installs, downloads, and so on. Many companies go public without being profitable, but no self-funded company stays afloat without profit.

Why Is Profit Important to Your Employee Experience?

According to Amplio Digital founder and CEO Marshall Hayes, self-funded companies tend to be more frugal and make decisions that will benefit the company in both the short- and long-term. In funded companies, it's more important to focus on long-term growth. According to Hayes, funded companies "make more decisions in general; they try many things, then figure out fast whether they succeed or fail. Self-funded companies need to move fast and be cautious."

In a self-funded company, the focus on profitability can be a liability for startup employees.

"If you have external cash and you don't have to be profitable, your primary metric is growth, which means you need to keep as many people as possible and reduce turnover," says ADP Senior Director of Customer Experience Nicolle Paradise. "In self-funded companies, your primary metric is profitability, so to maintain those numbers, headcount (operational expenditure or OpEx) is the first to get cut in lieu of capital expenditure (CapEx)."

A nonprofitable funded company may be unsuccessful in their next round, and therefore your job may be on the line. In a self-funded company, you have to pay attention to both profit and the growth metrics you should be hitting. In a self-funded company, if you're not profitable for more than a month at a time, that's a real problem. Funded companies can often run without profit for a long time. Some funded companies run unprofitably for their entire existence before they're acquired (or go under). But if you work for a self-funded or funded company, pay attention to the financial goals of the company and work hard to ensure they are being hit. If they're not, look around for other job opportunities.

If your self-funded company never raises funding, you'll likely be doing everything on a shoestring, especially in marketing and sales, because most revenue has to be invested into building the product, platform, or software.

When working for a self-funded company, you'll learn how to work leaner and smarter. But you may also face a lot of frustration. Self-funded companies may be tightly held, meaning the founder is very involved in the company. That's a difficult scenario if you aren't aligned with the founder. Funded companies can fire the CEO and are beholden to a board. Some self-funded companies still have boards, but usually it's one founder or several founders who hold all of the power.

According to website *Financial Samurai*, there are clear benefits to joining a funded company. There is a lower likelihood of failure, your base salary will be higher, and the company "has probably established a scalable business model to potentially allow you to cash in on your equity. If you were one of the first few employees and got closer to 5% equity, that level would be much more aligned with the risk you are taking."[17]

Fundraising Stages

Typically, startups with less than $5M in funding are considered "early stage." They're probably either in Seed Funding or pre-Series A round. Funding rounds are when startups obtain investment from venture capital or other investment sources. If they are self-funded—aka bootstrapped—they must be profitable. But venture-funded startups do not need to be profitable; for many reasons they primarily need to grow. The earlier the company, the greater the risk and reward.

According to VC Jason Lemkin, "Employee experience is very different under $10m in Annual Recurring Revenue (ARR). If the company is self-funded, things are slower, and can feel 'cheap.' But the experience is also more empowering. It normalizes after $10m ARR."[18]

Understand Your Startup's Fundraising Goals

Startup veteran Matt Hessler advocates learning what your company's fundraising goals are before signing on.

Ask the hiring manager about "use of proceeds" if your company did take venture money. Depending on how transparent the culture is, they should be able to give a general statement of "why did you take the money and what did you use it to do?" That might give you an interesting indication of company goals and trajectory. If it is, "We took this capital and our use of proceeds is going to be to expand our sales efforts internationally," how might that affect your role as a hire? Outside forces like VCs and new board members might be leaning on the exec team to do whatever they promised they would do with the proceeds from raising capital. Asking about fundraising gives you perspective into the direction of the company.

I would be worried if I came from a company that did x and raised money and said "use of proceeds is to develop product y," as that says to me the core business is not great. It's not necessarily a huge red flag but with (now defunct startup) Trada, we were a search platform and used a certain amount of VC platform to extend our model into Facebook ads. That meant seeing potential opportunity but also limitations or issues with the core business.

If you're not sure of a company's funding status, the site crunchbase.com provides a helpful database of companies, their funding and investors, and information about their leadership.

Company Maturity

As the company matures during your tenure there, expect more process, structure, and rigidity—and usually predictability and stability. Over time, you'll have an automated process for submitting expense claims. You will be offered a 401k. You will have performance reviews. People are expected to actually show up to the office. When companies scale, they tend to embrace systems much more than when they're just starting out. For instance, GitHub started out with no managers and a flat structure. Then they grew, and suddenly they had some managers. Then they embraced some level of hierarchies within the company. In June 2018, GitHub was acquired by Microsoft, and now it may have a completely different structure.

The book *The Paypal Wars* tells the story of life at Paypal from the perspective of Eric M. Jackson, an early employee, who joined without a clear role. At that early stage he was able to contribute massive value while navigating periods of change, through mergers, office changes, and more. Do you want to work for a company that is more chaotic and has less structure? If you dislike structure and process, you may want to leave a company as it grows to the stages where it starts implementing these things.

Benefits of Working for Early-Stage Tech Companies

In the early days, everything is greenfield. You may get a leadership role early on, since there are fewer people. There are more opportunities for stock to be worth something and to get in on the action earlier. If you don't mind frequent chaos, early-stage companies can be a marvelous place to grow and learn.

Benefits of Working for More Mature Companies

Mature startups offer health insurance, more robust HR policies, clear pathways to success, and sometimes (though not always) less risk (though less reward too). There is also the potential for clearer career paths. For example, when Google was a fledgling startup, it had little structure. Now Google has clearly defined rungs on its career ladder. Google has a leveling system for engineers; if you are L3 (entry level, also known as Software Engineer II) you can research what's needed to become L4 (Software Engineer III). These levels are consistent across the organization.

Facebook and other large companies have comparable rungs. At another startup, you could move up more quickly through the ranks, but it is likely that you will have to participate in the process of defining what the next rank is. If you want to have a clear sense of how to level up with the added benefits of predictability and stability, a more mature startup may be a better fit for you.

Assessing Company Financing and Overall Maturity

As you're considering where to work, company financing is an important part of the picture. Sometimes startups are so early they are "pre-product," in which case you'll want to know when they expect to get their product to market. Find out what funding is available to enable the launch of the product to market. If the startup has already launched their tech into the market, do they have "product-market" fit?

If you can, find out about their burn rate (how much cash they are spending each month). Ask the founder or research online how much financing they've had. (A quick Google search should return results in many cases.) It can be an imprecise science, but get a sense of their financial stability—will they run out of money in three months or three years? While assessing a startup's finances, look for indicators that there is or will be traction in the market, that the company values frugality while still investing in their team and market opportunities, and that it has predictable revenue or at least a clear path to it.

Geography

Discussions about the emerging tech scenes outside of the heart of the tech world, Silicon Valley, usually center around the following issues:

- How founders and employees stand to benefit or suffer depending on where their company is headquartered
- How accessible capital is to founders based outside Silicon Valley ("the Valley")
- Recruiting and retaining talent outside the Valley
- Whether startups can be competitive despite their distance from Sand Hill Road, an infamous arterial home to many venture capital firms in the Valley

From an employee perspective, little formal advice has been given in terms of whether we need to build our careers within the Valley bubble or if we can be successful entirely (or mostly) outside of it.

Startup Life in the Valley: A (Very Cursory) Primer

Silicon Valley has become the epicenter of the startup world. Much has been said about it as a locus for so-called tech "genius." Eric Weiner, author of *The Geography of Genius*, writes:

Like living in LA if you're in the film industry, living in the Valley is a no-brainer if you're interested in being around some of the brightest minds working on some of the most interesting problems in tech. The Valley boasts some of the more iconic aspects of tech culture: the big commuter busses shuttling people from one end of the Peninsula to the other; turnover like nobody's business; and, of course, venture capital pouring into new ideas.[19]

As Hollywood is for film or New York for finance and fashion, Silicon Valley is undeniably the epicenter of all things tech. As a result, Silicon Valley draws people from all over the world specifically to work in tech. If you work for a more mature startup, buses with Wi-Fi may shuttle you to and from work so you don't have to miss a moment of productivity.

Working in Silicon Valley has its pros and cons:

- **It is home to some of the greatest tech talent and companies in the world.** If you want to work with leaders in the field, or at cutting-edge companies, look no further. It is also home to Stanford University and University of California, Berkeley, as well as many other excellent institutions focused on startups, technology, and innovation.

- **It can be hard to live a balanced life.** Most people in tech are commuting in significant traffic and working longer hours in Silicon Valley than other places. As a result, you may not meet people outside the industry as easily, and you may spend the majority of your life focused on work. You can work around this, but it's the dominant culture.

• **It is expensive.** While tech affords greater incomes and benefits than many other industries, the San Francisco Bay Area (the larger encompassing region around San Francisco that is focused on tech) is notoriously expensive. For current and future parents, note that expenses like daycare are much higher than average.

Startups Beyond Silicon Valley

While it's true that much of the world's technology is designed (if not built) in Silicon Valley, there's a growing trend toward thriving tech hubs outside the Valley. Places such as Boulder, Colorado, Salt Lake City, Utah, and Austin, Texas, are prominent for the startup community, and many investors are pouring resources into companies all over the country. Brad Feld's book *Startup Communities* is a great resource to understand more about how startup ecosystems function and how to get involved in one near you if you're not in Silicon Valley.

You Don't Have to Move to the Bay to
Have an Awesome Startup Career

You might assume you'll have to move to Silicon Valley to have a successful career in tech. In fact, geographies outside the SF Bay Area can be immensely rewarding for those looking to work for a company based around a local industry. For instance, Washington, D.C., boasts great opportunities for those wanting to work in tech around the political machine; Denver, Colorado, is leading the way for cannabis tech companies; Seattle, Washington, is home to e-commerce giant Amazon; New York is the epicenter for media-ecosystem tech; LA is where to go for entertainment industry tech.

Focus on the values and other criteria that are important to you in a tech position and career, and if living somewhere other than the Valley makes sense, there's no reason to move there arbitrarily. That being said, you may want to strongly consider attending conferences in the Bay Area or plan trips there to meet with industry leaders at least once a year if you can swing it. Just because the Valley is the undeniable epicenter of the tech world, it doesn't mean you have to physically live there year-round to be successful in tech.

Place Matters

Startup culture in Salt Lake City is markedly different from startup culture in Kuala Lumpur. The city and country in which you are working will impact your experience dramatically, even if it's at the same company—take particular note if you're considering transferring office locations.

How to Decide Whether to Work for a Startup Outside Silicon Valley

What Kind of Lifestyle Are You Looking for?

It is increasingly possible to work remotely (i.e., not at a company's office) for a company based in the Bay Area and live, well, anywhere in the world. I lived and worked in Boulder, Colorado, and worked for a Bay Area tech company, traveling to visit their office quarterly.

Things that can be helpful to think about:

- Do you work or want to work in an emerging area of tech that you think will be most cutting-edge in the Bay Area (for example, working on VR tech)?

- Where do you and your family want to live? Is being in or near a specific location (family, a spouse's job) crucial?
- What is your commute tolerance?
- Do you like the Bay Area for reasons other than tech (i.e., the weather, the nature, the culture)?

If the company is distributed in multiple locations, find out during your interview if you will be placed somewhere other than the primary HQ. Are remote employees treated as less important than in-office employees, receiving fewer benefits and getting edged out of important meetings or assignments? Find out if one office is specific to a particular function (for example, engineers in one place, sales in another). If you're not a salesperson, working in a predominantly sales office might be a bit jolting (expect to overhear a lot of phone calls!). Spend time talking to employees who work in various company locations to gain a better understanding of what your office environment will be like.

As a former remote employee at ServiceRocket, a self-funded business-to-business (B2B) tech startup headquartered in Palo Alto, I felt valued when efforts were made to include me, even though I was many miles away from my team. I never felt "lesser than" because conscious efforts were made to include me, including providing a "beam" (a remote-controlled iPad-like robot that enabled me to motor around the office from anywhere in the world), ensuring that all work was done "out loud" to enable effective team collaboration without being in the same physical location.

The company's many offices were also unified through our shared values. While the offices had different cultures, you'd find some of the same traits among employees throughout the world. Our company emphasized teamwork through our shared value "thinking team," which meant that whether in Santiago or Sydney, we prioritized being helpful and supportive of one another.

Startup Life Outside Silicon Valley: Spotlight on Boulder, Colorado

Boulder, Colorado, is a great place to launch a startup career by many measures. Local VC funds, accelerators, mentors, and more provide lots of opportunities for prospective employees to join exciting startups and grow their careers. Learn more about the startup community in Boulder in Brad Feld's book *Startup Communities*.

A caveat: if you want to work for a "big-name" tech company that is headquartered in the Bay Area, you may need to move there or at least be willing to travel to their HQ frequently. If you work for Google's Boulder, Colorado, office, for example, you may be expected to make trips to Mountain View, California, occasionally or perhaps frequently.

For me, living in Boulder, experiencing a culture of giving before receiving, and working remotely for a company based in Silicon Valley with offices worldwide, was gratifying and felt like the best of both worlds. Later I decided to take a role at another tech company headquartered in Silicon Valley; I relocated there, returning to Boulder and Denver frequently to mentor at Techstars, a renowned startup accelerator. I also return for Boulder and Denver Startup Week and other events.

The choice is highly individual, but don't assume that the Bay Area is your only real option. In many cases, no matter where you work and live full-time, you will likely find ample reason to travel to Silicon Valley for conferences and networking.

Living and Working Outside the US

If you work for a startup with an international presence, you may have the opportunity to work outside the US either temporarily or for a prolonged stint. For example, at ServiceRocket, employees frequently have the opportunity to travel between the Palo Alto, Santiago, Kuala Lumpur, and Sydney offices. Each office has its own culture and norms, and short-term work experiences offer employees the chance to live and work in a new culture without having to move permanently. Then again, if you do want to transfer to an entirely new city, sometimes your US-based company will allow it, usually after a certain time period of working in the US HQ. When joining a startup with an international presence, ask about transfer and travel opportunities during the interview process.

Spotlight: Riga, Latvia

Entrepreneur Sandijs Ruluks lives and works in Riga, Latvia. He shared with me his thoughts on the startup scene in Riga:

> For those who work on global products, Riga is great. In a lot of ways, it's easier to focus on the company without being distracted with the big city life. The community in Riga is split in two parts—younger companies that are happy to share everything they know, and older companies

that aren't sharing much and live in their own worlds. At the same time, people are moving between these worlds, and word travels fast. [Our startup] works out of a co-working space, The Mill (millriga.com), which we actually co-founded. Part of the space is dedicated to public events, so most meetups in Riga happen in our space. At some point, having our own office would make sense, of course, but currently the benefit of working together with other cool startups outweighs that.

I asked Sandijs, "What are the differences between working in Riga and working in Silicon Valley?" He responded:

Riga is known for its developer talent. We have lots of really smart people around. On the other hand, the Valley is full of sales and marketing people and, of course, the money. Therefore we go there for things we can't get here, and it is typical to travel there a few times a year.

CHAPTER THREE

STARTUP CULTURE AND VALUES

Culture and values, related to company maturity and size, majorly impact your experience working at a startup. This chapter discusses different kinds of startup culture and values and offers ideas for helping you find the right place.

Personal and Workplace Values

According to a study reported in the *New York Times,* "One of the most important dimensions of job satisfaction is how you feel about your employer's mission."[20] Robert H. Frank, an economics professor at Cornell University, reports that equal incomes may produce significantly higher life satisfaction if the person aligns with the mission and values of their workplace. "When most people leave work each evening, they feel better if they have made the world better in some way, or at least haven't made it worse."[21] This especially applies to millennials. A recent *New York Times Magazine* piece reports, "Survey after survey shows that millennials want to work for companies that place a premium on employee welfare, offer flexible scheduling, and above all, bestow a sense of purpose."[22]

Where we work and the nature of our work greatly impacts our life satisfaction. We owe it to ourselves to find a startup that aligns with our values and will enable us to produce our best work.

Company decisions are driven by values. These values color everything from what the office looks like on Friday afternoon to how customers are treated. When evaluating whether a startup is right for you, understand the company values and how they align with your own.

Startup Values: What Are They, Really?

Each startup operates within an implicit or explicit value system; this is the set of principles that guide every aspect of the business and will deeply shape your experience working at a company.

Values help companies orient and make decisions when they reach impasses. The company's values provide an answer to the question: "Does this align with what we want to achieve?" and should be consulted before proceeding with any major decision.

Company Values Drive Behavior

Whether implicit or explicit, these values shape company behavior. They encompass hiring, firing, how employees are treated, the kind of office environments fostered, the formality of employee attire, philosophies toward customers, parental leave policies, the kind of products built, how products are marketed and sold, and so much more. Company values shape every experience you will have at a startup. Here are a few examples of stated company values:

- Talk straight. (ServiceRocket)
- Results first, substance over flash. (Rackspace)
- Focus on the user and all else will follow. (Google)
- Deliver WOW Through Service. (Zappos)
- Respect for the Individual. (Accenture)
- Take Work But Not Ourselves seriously. (Kapost)
- Feel Free. (Twitter)
- Judgement. (Netflix)

According to Netflix CEO Reed Hastings, "The actual company values, as opposed to the nice-sounding values, are shown by who gets rewarded, promoted or let go."[23] Netflix is known for its strictly enforced culture code, which is publicly available through their "culture manifesto" on the web.

The disjointed relationship between values and behavior is exemplified through a famous example of corporate fraud, Enron, which stated in their lobby values like "integrity, respect, and communication" that clearly did not translate into company-wide behavior. These values, as the Enron example illustrate, mean nothing without corresponding actions.

In almost every case, unless you're working with a very early-stage company, the values will be explicitly stated. But how can you tell if a company lives its values? Consider asking these questions before joining a startup:

- "How are values carried out or "lived" at this company, and how is that measured?"

- "When has the leadership team had to make a difficult decision in order to stay true to company values, and what was the impact to both the company and the employees?"

Many companies state values that sound great, but actually allow for toxic behavior. "Above all, win," sounds nice, but it could leave the door open for jerks to be gainfully employed—as long as they "crush it." If there's a stated company value that sounds fishy or nebulous, you'd be wise to ask questions. Don't accept vague answers or leave without concrete stories and examples of how values are put into practice—or prepare to be disappointed.

It's important to note that even startups that fail to define their values (again, most often very early-stage companies) have them—they're just implicit. Any company that doesn't *explicitly* state its values is more likely to operate under values they would be embarrassed to put to proverbial paper. Says Hastings, "Real company values are the behaviors and skills that we particularly value in fellow employees."

For example, among their nine values, Netflix explains that "Judgement" looks like this in practice:

Judgement
- You make wise decisions (people, technical, business, and creative) despite ambiguity
- You identify root causes, and get beyond treating symptoms

- You think strategically, and can articulate what you are, and are not, trying to do
- You smartly separate what must be done well now, and what can be improved later[24]

Values at Early-Stage Startups

Early-stage startups are the least likely to state values but are, of course, still guided by values, albeit ones that are implicit or by default. A company made up of just two co-founders, for example, may not be mature enough to have created a fancy presentation deck like Netflix, but perhaps they created the company to perpetuate the good ol' days of university where they met.

If you are thinking of working for a very early-stage company, ask them if the leadership team regularly discusses their values—and if you'd be joining the leadership team, ask them if you can be part of these sessions before going all-in. Also, expect early-stage startups to pivot quite a lot and, as a result, potentially change their values and culture. If a startup starts out serving bankers, but then pivots when they realize their real customer base is high school-level educators, the values and culture may change as a result (though, of course, not necessarily).

At Fog Creek Software, founder Joel Spolsky baked values into his company even before it began. He says that in addition to the "Smart and Gets Things Done" hiring ethos, which amounts to hiring people who—you guessed it—are competent and execute, it was imperative not to hire any jerks. He said that even before they started the company (read: early on in the startup), they realized they should add the rule "Not a Jerk." Joel says this differed from his experience working at Microsoft, because he felt that although Microsoft purported to hire nice people, being a jerk would not be grounds for disqualification from a job or promotion there.

"This doesn't seem to really hurt from a business perspective, although it does hurt from a recruiting perspective. Who wants to work at a company where jerks are tolerated?" he says in his book *Smart & Gets Things Done*.[25] This is a great example because it shows that early-stage startups can choose to establish values and enforce them even before companies exist. Spolsky says that social values make an impact on a company's ability to recruit great developers.

Know Thyself

Natalie Baumgartner, PhD, a business psychologist expert on the topic of employee-company alignment and founder of employee engagement startup RoundPegg, says "fit" is one of the most important aspects of your career success.

As Baumgartner and her team developed RoundPegg, their research showed that everyone has a core wiring that makes up inherent aspects of who we are as individuals—i.e., our core values. While people have the capacity to change, Baumgartner's research shows we don't change much. By the time we hit eighteen and enter the work world, much of our wiring is set, and it doesn't differ much over the course of our lives.

Our core values are different from our skills, abilities, and competencies. These influence how we behave in the world and thrive in places that align with our core values and essence. To figure out your own core values, Baumgartner suggests determining first who you are and gaining clarity about how you tick and what matters most to you. There are many ways to assess this: personality tests, quizzes, assessments, and coaches, but the key is to get curious and "know thyself." This can also help you as you manage others on a startup team.

Here are a few examples of personal assessments commonly used in the startup world:

- DISC profiles
- Myers-Briggs Type Indicator
- Enneagram
- StrengthsFinder
- Personal Values Assessment

(Note: while I personally find each of the above assessments to be useful for building cohesive teams, some of these are not scientifically validated.)

Understanding ourselves, what we value, and how we operate on teams is important. There is a body of literature discussing personalities and how to build effective teams that balance skills and weaknesses. In the work world, many of us believe we need to subvert some aspect of who we are for our work. We fear we won't be accepted or desirable if we choose a place that doesn't align with who we are.

The next step is to understand any organization you're joining; do your homework by learning how the organization truly operates. Baumgartner says there's no single right culture: you just have to find that fit.

If a company doesn't state values around something you care about, that doesn't necessarily mean they don't champion them. But it is less likely to be a priority. On the flip side, a company may state a value but not actually take actions that reflect it. No matter the maturity or stage, look for a startup that incorporates values you care about into every decision.

Ask about a company's values during the interview process.
Research ahead of time what values the company states on their website, and then ask how they are actually lived and measured at the company. What was a difficult decision the startup made in order to stay true to one of their values? Listen for stories that include plenty of details. You'll quickly get a sense of whether the values hold meaning or are just there for show.

"I think it's important to ensure your values are aligned with company and founder as much as possible," says Hiten Shah. "It's talking to founders and being able to be clear about what you want out of a situation and what your values are and whether they align with founders or not. That can only come from testing."

Startup Cultures
Startup values affect startup cultures, and these vary widely by office, department, and team. Within a local office, there are often many subcultures, because each new hire shapes a company's environment. If they have been hired according to the company's values (see above), there will be room for many kinds of cultures that align with the values.

Is It Bro-y?

Whether by intention or not, many startups have cultivated "bro" cultures that involve Ping-Pong balls, Nerf gun fights, beer carts, and other stereotypically "frat" behavior at best, and hostile behavior and outright discrimination toward women and other underrepresented people at worst. Increasingly, big tech companies such as Uber and Google have come under fire for perpetuating cultures that are unwelcoming and even discriminatory toward women and minorities. For more on this topic, Emily Chang's *Brotopia* is a great book on understanding bro culture in tech startups.

Diversity and Inclusivity (D&I)

Diversity and inclusivity (often referred to in the industry as D&I) are gaining attention lately in the media, especially for startups under fire for lacking them. The term refers to a company's initiatives to foster a heterogeneous and supportive work environment. D&I has gotten a lot of press in the past few years because so many of the major tech companies—including Google, Twitter, and Facebook—are still homogeneous (predominantly white, cisgender, heterosexual men), especially at the highest levels of leadership, even after spending millions on improving the lack of diversity in tech.

So, What Is D&I?

At its core, D&I is about everyone being able to be themselves at work. According to entrepreneur and community builder Mandy Godown, the "inclusivity" piece of D&I is the part that matters most.

The goal shouldn't be diversity for its own sake. It should be inclusivity, indicative of a healthy culture where people feel welcome to bring themselves as they are because of who they are. Inclusivity means being a welcome part of that community. On paper, a company could have a lot of gender diversity, but you may find it's only in the lower levels of the company. That sends a strong message about whether it's truly inclusive. True inclusivity means having diverse groups of people at all levels of the company.

As Mandy says, there are fewer women, LGBTQ people, and people of color in positions of leadership at startups. While organizations like Backstage Capital and Cowboy Ventures are changing things, this trend also remains in leadership at venture capital firms.

Should you be the "one and only" person like you at your startup, don't despair—you can stay (and *should* if you want to!). Ideally your company is open to working on D&I and will take a look at its practices, including hiring and culture, that may be impacting its lack of diversity.

What should you do if your company doesn't want to work on D&I or isn't doing so fast enough? Here is my advice: Go. Seriously. There are enough startups now that care about this *and* are solving important, interesting problems. You needn't work somewhere that is stuck in the past!

As an openly queer woman, I have consistently come out at work before joining a company, and I have worked for startups that prioritize D&I. Before joining BuildingConnected, I came out to both of the founders during our interviews, gauging their interest in cultivating an LGBTQ-friendly environment for their employees. I deeply resonated with the statement on BuildingConnected's career page:

> We reject the status quo. We challenge the norms of tech and construction, and we believe that both industries benefit from a more diverse workplace that includes talented women, people of color, and the LGBTQ community.[26]

While a statement on a career page doesn't guarantee anything, it goes a long way toward indicating that you're joining a place where everyone can be themselves at work.

Sometimes, no matter how inclusive a company attempts to be, we often feel we have to project a certain persona at work. This is true even at startups. There can be pressure to feel like you have to know all the answers, or act a certain way, especially if you're a member of a marginalized group.

Sarah Innocenzi says she was drawn to startups because they afforded her the opportunity to be herself all the time.

> It was the first time in my career I could just be me. It gives me chills thinking about it. Large companies have societies of their own and it's exhausting to be someone else when you're there. I can now put all of my energy into making a company great.

Ethnic and Racial Diversity

How inclusive is a tech company in terms of racial and ethnic diversity? Many larger tech companies have employee resource groups (ERG)s. These voluntary working groups organize to foster a more inclusive workplace aligned with business objectives and values. Twitter has BlackBirds; Salesforce has Blackforce. Being in the minority can be lonely. At your company, you need to decide if the environment works for you. If you do stay, get support outside of your company from a local meetup or national group.

LGBTQ Awareness

Are gender-nonconforming employees valued? Can you transition on the job? Are there internal LGBTQ groups? In Boulder, I founded Flatirons LGBTQ Tech Meetup to help companies become more inclusive. Organizations such as StartOut, Lesbians Who Tech, and others are focused on increasing LGBTQ awareness.

Cross-Cultural Awareness

At Facebook, during Ramadan they provide takeaway containers so employees can bring their meal home with them to consume after fasting. Will you work for a company that expresses similar sensitivity to different cultures?

Accessibility

Can differently abled employees feel included? Is there appropriate accommodation with accessibility? What about for customers? Does the company create accessible products?

Diverse Leadership

Does leadership at a startup involve a diverse group, or is it homogeneous? Look for people from diverse backgrounds in leadership—including the board—as a good sign that a company is not hiring and promoting according to biases. Beware if you don't see this, even if other parts of the company are diverse, and don't be afraid to ask about it in an interview.

Strategies for Assessing Startup Culture Before Joining

Before working for a startup, it is essential to understand company culture and values to ensure you align with them. This is not a complete list, but here are some of the questions you should explore before joining any startup.

How Is Bias Handled?

All humans have biases. "We need to out our biases to ourselves and each other and not be afraid to say, 'I'm biased,'" says ServiceRocket COO Erin Rand. "We need to constantly remember and take action to correct our biases. We can't feel ashamed of our biases and let that shame prevent us from doing the right thing."

Given that bias is universal, how does the startup you're considering joining handle bias? Do they acknowledge bias openly, working to ensure that it isn't playing a role in key decisions such as hiring, promotions, and firing? Startups that acknowledge bias take steps to mitigate it. Those that sweep it under the rug reinforce bias.

Consider asking an interviewer to give you an example of how bias is addressed at the company. Their answer may be mere lip service, but you are more likely to find a place that genuinely takes bias seriously if you ask about it and receive an open, direct answer. Beware when anyone skirts the issue or says it "isn't an issue"; it's *always* an issue.

What Are Turnover Rates and How Do Departures Look at Your Startup?

Most startups have some degree of turnover, especially in junior roles in support and sales departments. Tech is also an industry where people tend to move around, and hiring managers and recruiters don't judge people for hopping around as much as they do in other industries. This being said, some startups have far more turnover than others. The key things to look at when it comes to turnover are whether people are fleeing a particular department in higher numbers (e.g., if you discover no salesperson stays in a role for more than three months, you may want to steer clear) and whether people who stay are rewarded for their tenure or get relegated into roles without a clear growth path.

Before joining, ask how long people stay at the company and see how representatives respond. If they dance around it and give excuses for why people leave frequently, be on the alert for other indicators that there are major issues. If they are proud that people stay on board, that's a good sign—but remember to also see if people who stay get promoted, get to take on exciting new roles and challenges, and aren't just sticking around slowly becoming irrelevant.

How do departures look at the startup where you work? Before you join, ask about the employee exit experience. If employees leave and then sometimes come back, that's a good sign. If departing employees leave behind a trail of awful Glassdoor reviews, take notice.

"It can be helpful to bring a few polarizing comments about the company from Glassdoor to the interview," says Nicolle Paradise. "Ask what the interviewer finds true and untrue about the sentiment and why."

It's also worth finding out if your company offers a decent severance package for employees who are laid off or fired.

Some startups advertise their severance packages. Netflix, for instance, has an outstanding severance package for employees. They do this to make it easier for managers to fire underperformers or bad fits. The mentality is that if you're firing someone who you know is going to have a great parting experience, you're more likely to do so rather than keeping employees who aren't a fit, thus ultimately improving the quality of the team.

Unexpected or unwanted departures can happen for all kinds of reasons at startups; sometimes a startup hired someone too quickly, or no longer needs a person or department after a pivot. Your role as an employee is to make yourself as versatile and adaptable as possible, but nonetheless you may depart either willingly or unwillingly, and you want to make sure that it will be as positive an experience as possible.

What Is the Dress Code?

Dressing for success at a startup can mean anything from jeans and a logo t-shirt to khakis and a button-down shirt. Ask ahead before an interview—nothing looks worse than being overdressed or underdressed. The key consideration is: will you, in all of your uniqueness, feel comfortable bringing your whole self to work? If you have multiple piercings and your hair is dyed a color that does not naturally grow on human heads, will you feel out of place? Is there a policy you can't live with? Do you prefer to dress up and wish to work somewhere where this is the expectation? Find out ahead of time by talking to HR and looking at the company's social media pages and website.

Does the Company Champion Inclusivity?

Tech still has a long way to go in terms of diversity and inclusivity. The latest reports show that startups are overwhelmingly white male-dominated.[27] This is a big can of worms; many companies purport to champion inclusivity, but what does this mean?

How to Answer These Questions

Do your online research. If a startup's career video, proudly displayed on their homepage, showcases men hitting each other with Nerf guns after downing sake bombs celebrating a release of code, well, there you have it. Does the company have "Best Place to Work" awards, or is their Glassdoor page rife with one-star reviews highlighting the terrible leadership team from disgruntled former employees? Note: ex-employee reviews may not be all true. Look for patterns.

In addition to the company website and sites like Glassdoor, don't miss company social media accounts, especially if they have an Instagram; that tends to be the least formal platform with posts most indicative of culture. Peruse social accounts of company employees—especially those who will be on your team. As an aside, be mindful of the way you personally interact on social media; startups can and will research you too!

Talk to people. The best way to figure out what a company is really like is to talk to people who are currently working there. You can also talk to former employees. Try to engage people who aren't directly involved in your hiring decision. When you go for the interview, observe. Hang out. And . . .

Go to the kitchen. Pretend you're an anthropologist on a mission to observe the startup culture through its kitchen. Go get a glass of water and listen to what is being said. Sample the startup's snacks and see if they're organic/gluten-free/free-range enough for your taste. Overhear how employees are feeling about their work and lives. Do they clean up after themselves? Analiese Brown, Director of Talent and Culture at CampMinder, wrote a great blog on the link between employee engagement and kitchen cleanliness.[28] You will invariably learn something if you spend time in the canteen.

Observe leaders—and lower-level employees. Even if you're considering an executive position—or perhaps especially—pay close attention to how the company treats those who aren't in management. This includes those fresh out of college and those in lower-level positions. Respect for everyone should be a foundation of any company culture, and if it's not, you can anticipate other problems.

Be a consultant. Some startups will hire you as a consultant on a project basis before you join full-time. This can be a great opportunity to truly understand the work environment, as well as how likely you are to enjoy the experience.

Being a consultant is a great way to de-risk your involvement with a startup. You can engage in an initial project with a company in order to assess how you fit with the team you'll be working with, see whether the values are truly lived by the company, and whether you and the company/role are a match overall.

Some companies have employees do an unpaid test or assignment before joining. This is *not* the same thing as being a consultant! It's one-sided and doesn't quite give you the chance to dive in with a team, whereas with consulting, you'll be contributing something tangible, be paid for your work, and get a much better insider's view of the business. Not every company will allow you to do this, but it's worth asking if it may be possible to do an initial engagement prior to working together.

CHAPTER FOUR

EVALUATING YOUR FIT

Choosing a Startup That's Right for You

Startups vary exponentially based on size, maturity, location, founding team, company values, and more. As with any job, you should assess whether a startup opportunity is right for you. At a large, public company, it is easier to understand financial health based on publicly available data. (Of course, large companies can experience volatility as well.) At a startup, this is not the case. Venture-funded companies that have lavish offices and catered lunches—external signals that times are flush—may in reality be on the brink of failure.

Identify what's most important to you and ask questions to ensure the startup opportunity you're assessing aligns with your priorities. By prioritizing what's important, you are more likely to get what you want, or skip an experience that won't be the right fit for you.

Here are some questions you should keep in mind as you assess startup fit.

What Are the Company's Long-Term Goals?

Is the company planning to scale rapidly? Are they planning to go public or get acquired? Plans change, but it can't hurt to ask. If you want to work for a smaller startup with fifty people, and this startup is on a rocket ship to scale fast and/or get acquired, you should know that upfront. If you don't know whether you want to work for a larger company or not, that's OK.

Is This a Good Career Move for Me?

Will you have the opportunity to build a practice, hire a team, and do work you're excited about? Many factors impact your experience at a startup, and you'll need to constantly reevaluate whether it is a good fit.

Is the Company Financially Stable?

Your contribution to a startup is an investment; like a venture capitalist or any other investor, you should care about getting a return. You take on risk when joining, and the better you understand the financials of a company prior to joining, the more confident you can be that you're joining a startup headed in a positive growth trajectory. You'll have to do some digging to find this information for non-publicly traded companies (which, at that point, aren't really startups).

A startup may appear to be doing well, having raised a big fundraising round or gotten a ton of press in tech media, but it may be spending tons of money on a flashy office while failing to attract and retain business. The burn rate—how fast the startup burns resources—is something to look out for. Frugality balanced with smart investments in the right areas, whether for a self-funded or VC-backed company, is what you should be looking for.

Has the Company Achieved Product-Market Fit?

How clear is the company's vision of who is going to buy your software or platform? How will it be monetized, if it isn't being monetized already? If the company isn't profitable, are they on an upward trajectory with their growth goals? It's OK to join pre-product/market fit, but know that you'll be coming in very early in that case.

Is the Company Solving a Problem You Care About (or at Least Are Vaguely Interested in)?

Technology startups solve many different kinds of problems. A startup may have achieved product-market fit, is riding a rocket user growth trajectory, has the best team ever, super cool offices in a great location . . . but if you don't care at all about the problem the company solves for their customers and partners, you might not be happy. Trust me: it will make the work a lot harder, and potentially even downright unbearable, if you're spending all of your time solving a problem you don't think is important. Are you solving a problem that matters to you personally, or at least that you know matters a lot to your target market?

A caveat to consider: don't discount a problem that's being solved as one you can't care about just because you don't *currently* care about it (or didn't before joining).

Dustin DeVan is co-founder of BuildingConnected, a tech company that serves the preconstruction industry, a previously underserved market. DeVan had construction industry experience prior to founding his company. But many who have joined (yours truly included!) didn't know a thing about construction, then came to care about the target markets and problems being solved for them after learning more and joining. I personally find it gratifying to help people do their jobs better and find more work more efficiently.

Sometimes working in a new sphere can be refreshing. You may find working on problems that directly impact customers in a space previously underserved by technology to be much more exciting than, say, making someone's meal arrive five minutes faster or a salesperson's job 4 percent more efficient. That being said, there is nothing wrong with meal delivery or sales workflow optimization work! The important thing is to identify what matters to you, and do some exploration beforehand to ensure you're aligned with the company.

How Does the Startup Feel about Their Competitors?

Before joining a startup, you should have a good understanding of how the company thinks about and behaves around their competitors. Are they aware of competition but focused on their own path? Do they obsess about competitors? All startups have competition; most operate somewhere in between "ignore competitors" and "unleash all hell" on them. If they are ruthless towards competition—maybe even doing things that border on illegality—you should learn that in advance and decide whether you're comfortable with their tactics.

Research the CEO/Exec Team on Glassdoor, LinkedIn, or Another Site

Researching the leadership team online should be one of the

first things you do when considering a new opportunity. How does the CEO present herself online? Do they seem like the kind of leader you'd want to follow? Do their social media posts represent them and the company well? In today's political climate, some want to see that the CEO or co-founders are posting socially minded things in addition to things about the company. If you care about this, you'll want to do research. If the CEO is highly rated on Glassdoor, meaning people seem to believe in their leadership, that's a great sign. Take negative reviews with a grain of salt; again, you're not looking for outliers—you want to understand the trend and whether it's headed in the right direction.

How Not to Get Scammed

If a startup sounds too good to be true, it just might be. Some startups aren't as good as they seem—even VC-funded companies who have ostensibly been vetted can have major issues. Especially when joining a less-established startup, do as much research as you can on the founding team and company financials.

Confirmation bias is the phenomenon of seeking information that reinforces what we already believe to be true. If you really want to work at a company, you may be tempted to overlook the realities. It's OK to be excited, and you may decide to overlook flaws and issues, but if they are present when you're first hired, there will *always* be an issue down the line, so try to do your research as objectively as possible. Issues are OK; again, all startups have them. The key is to be aware of them in advance and to choose to work there anyway. Due diligence upfront makes a big difference.

Will I Work on Meaningful Things and Will
That Work Actually See the Light of Day?

Consultant and entrepreneur Samuel Hulick recommends finding out whether what you are working on building or selling actually gets shipped to customers.

"Will you work on features that are killed before they stand a chance? If most of the things you're working on never get shipped, that may get frustrating," says Hulick.

Will the Overall Situation of This Startup,
Including Its Team and This Role, Fulfill Me?

Many things influence your happiness at a startup, and this can and will fluctuate over time. The question to ask yourself is: "With everything I know about this startup, the role, and the people with whom I will work, can I be successful *and* fulfilled?"

I like how startup veteran Matt Hessler thinks about this topic:

> Make sure that the role and day to day in the company is rewarding for you intellectually, emotionally, spiritually. That is super important. Don't expect there will be a big pot of gold.

Advice from a VC: Finding the Right Startup Fit

Venture capitalist Brad Feld has worked with dozens of startups and advises thinking carefully about culture, fit, and personal growth when evaluating startup opportunities. He is an expert at helping create alignment between people and companies (and funders). Feld says:

Look for companies and roles that match your experience and background, and look for a position where your strengths and weaknesses work well. Find out about company norms. Will it be a fun place to work? Will you be excited? Think about what kinds of dynamics there are from day to day.

PART TWO

CONTRIBUTE AND GROW

Working in a startup is not like being an employee elsewhere. Roles are often more flexible, responsibilities more ambiguous. The successful contributor at a startup is comfortable stepping up—and will grow as a result. The chapters in this section curate advice on how to take charge.

CHAPTER FIVE

FINDING YOUR ROLE

Generalist versus Specialist

The earlier and smaller the startup, the more general roles tend to be. At the beginning, a founder often will take the helm for sales, marketing, HR, operations, and more, and then will delegate as she grows her business. That said, regardless of the maturity of the startup you join, you will likely be carving out your own role beyond your formal job description, so be prepared to move out of your designated lane.

By diagnosing needs and embracing new challenges in new areas of an early-stage startup, you'll have the opportunity to grow your career and perhaps even transition to a new role that excites you more. In my personal experience, observing and addressing a need in an area not perceived as within my purview has been fundamental to my career growth.

Generally speaking, the more mature the company, the more defined or specialized the roles. Companies tend to hire additional sales and marketing people after fundraising, or, if self-funded, they reach a point where growth is impossible without key players in those roles. Typically after a fundraising round, companies will hire more "senior" people—i.e.,

VPs to balance out the founder's weaknesses and/or add "maturity" to the business. Specialists are essential for scaling a startup because these people bring specific expertise required to take the business to the next level.

At the outset of a startup, a founder may run every single department (sales, marketing, HR, operations) but as the company matures, those responsibilities are delegated to other people. As companies mature, expect more structure and specialization within departments.

"If a company is five or six people, it's usually made up of generalists—most often engineers if it's a Bay Area startup," says Hiten Shah. At this point, Shah says the next hire is often a specialist to fill a role like marketing, sales, or product.

"Companies may hire engineers, too, but those are three roles that a company tends to need pretty fast," says Shah.

Product is the least likely next hire when a company is around six people, because usually the founder team does this. Shah suggests that when a company is young, you should fully understand what skills and roles are needed and then determine whether you have those skills or if you're willing to learn them.

Once a company exceeds single-digit employee count, specialization increases exponentially.

"At forty people, you're likely going to be joining in a very specific role," says Shah.

If you know the startup will scale fast, you'll need to discern whether you're the type of person who can grow with the company. Learning opportunities can be the best part of startups; you can scale with a company and enjoy financial, career, and personal growth opportunities.

"We've had people start in customer support who ended up being product managers within a two- to three-year period because they were willing to start early," says Hiten. "It was scale-up time."

The opportunity to grow with the company as it scales can be one of the best parts of working for startups. You can start in a generalist role when a company is a dozen people and take on more specific roles as it scales up.

If you enjoy many kinds of tasks and roles, you may be happiest in the earlier stages of a startup, when it requires many people in generalist roles. If that's true for you, you may want to move to another company once your startup begins to expand.

At early stages the trajectory is from generalist to specialist; at later stages, you remain a specialist or grow within your department. For example, many in sales start as sales development representatives (SDRs) and end up becoming sales reps or sales managers as a company scales.

Unlike corporate jobs, where growth is generally limited or predetermined, there is no real limit to how much you can grow in a startup role. And, in fact, personal growth is essential.

"You either grow or you become irrelevant to the company," says Shah.

When Specializing, Make Sure You Enjoy It

It is important to frequently try new roles that flex your skills and require you to grow and learn. You won't want to continue doing some of the things you try, even if you're good at them. Be careful not to get pigeonholed into doing work you're good at but don't enjoy. Staying in a role in which you're not particularly fulfilled simply because you're performing well can lead to job dissatisfaction and burnout.

I found myself at risk of this when I took over my company's voice of the customer (VOC) program. An open position had led to a need, and as my specialty was in customer success-driven marketing, it made sense for me to take it on. I enjoyed strategizing how to better survey customers and take action around positive and negative customer feedback, but after several months of doing mostly VOC, I realized I didn't enjoy the act of interviewing customers and writing reviews. I much preferred working on other areas of marketing. I was good at VOC, but that didn't mean I enjoyed it.

Eventually I hired someone else to execute this who actually enjoyed the process of interviewing customers, and I went back to doing other marketing strategy work. I felt much happier. Be mindful of working in a specialty just because you're good at it. This is a surprisingly common cause of burnout.

From Generalist to Specialist in Marketing: Carly's Story

SendGrid Vice President of Revenue Marketing Carly Brantz says transitioning from generalist to specialist was key to growing her career. After several years at Visual Numerics out of college, Brantz applied for a job on Craigslist with Return Path, a Colorado-based technology company. At the time Brantz joined, it had a workforce of only thirty, which has grown to several hundred today. She says:

> No matter what your position in startup marketing, you need to be adaptable, flexible, and open to working on

many different projects—writing collateral or working on AdWords, or doing HTML for website formatting and email template design.

While working at Return Path, Carly reported to a different vice president of marketing each year for six years. "At the time it felt terrible, but it actually taught me a lot," says Brantz. "We restructured the whole marketing group every year, and I was put in a new role each time." Because of the shuffling, Carly worked on product, demand generation, partner marketing, marketing automation, and more.

When she joined SendGrid, Carly was a multi-hat marketer with a wide range of responsibilities. She grew with the company, became more specialized, and eventually led the revenue marketing efforts of the company when it filed for initial public offering (IPO).

"As I hired my first few employees, they also helped across those different areas," says Carly. However, over time, she says those same people have grown into focusing more on specialty areas. This specialization made the team more well-rounded and able to execute in anticipation of SendGrid's IPO. Focusing on these separate functions made them more successful after the IPO as well. According to Carly:

> You're working on SEO right away, or content, or email. I would encourage people to think about what that specialty area is that they enjoy, that's interesting to them, as well as researching a wide range of roles so that they don't get stuck in one specialty area that isn't challenging or interesting.

Carly advises people to choose a role based on individual preference and what motivates them. Then, decide if you'd like to be working on a lot of different areas, or if you'd prefer to (mostly) stay within a niche.

Nontechnical Roles

While some technical skills will be beneficial along your startup journey, you don't have to be a coder to have an amazing tech career. I attended a liberal arts college and spent my undergraduate years preparing to be a journalist. I didn't even take marketing classes in college, much less any related to computer science. This isn't rare—many in the startup world come from liberal arts backgrounds.

Some interesting nontechnical startup roles include:

- Director of Sales
- Chief People Officer
- Social Media Marketing Specialist
- Graphic Designer
- Strategic Finance Analyst[29]

If you lack technical experience and would like to transition into a technical role in a startup, there's no dearth of opportunities for you to learn to code these days. But what if you want to apply the skills you already have (accounting, finance, content curation) to the startup world? You can absolutely do this. An in-depth exploration of all of the roles and opportunities in startups is beyond of the scope of this book; I highly recommend Jeffrey Bussgang's fantastic book

Entering StartUpLand; he does a great job explaining the different needs of a typical startup, including technical and nontechnical roles.

CHAPTER SIX

BE A STELLAR STARTUP EMPLOYEE

Hacking Yourself to Do Your Best Work

You are the only one in control of your own productivity at a startup. While you may have a manager, you likely won't have anyone telling you exactly what to do. Self-management is a critical skill for anyone interested in joining a startup. Many books have been written about how to become more productive: *Essentialism* by Greg McKeown, *Getting Things Done* by David Allen, and *The Power of Habit* by Charles Duhigg are great resources for figuring out how to manage yourself and increase your productivity.

While you must learn systems to manage yourself, hack your habits, and become more productive based on what works for you, it's also important to remember that being "productive" includes taking time to connect with colleagues, peers, and leaders in the industry. Relationships matter because this industry is built on teamwork, both internally at your company and throughout the greater industry. Relationships are the lifeblood of the startup ecosystem. If you're not out at events networking, or at least attending some events your startup sponsors, you're going to miss out. Balance doing the work with connecting with others.

Maximize Your Energy

When is your energy highest and lowest throughout a workday, and what activities both at work and outside of work energize or enervate you? If you know you're a night owl, see if you can arrange to come to work later and stay into the evening. If you're a morning person, orient your day to start work earlier. Most people lag in the middle of the day; that's a great time to take a break if you can.

Focus on Solving Problems

If you work for a startup, you're going to spend a lot of your time solving problems. Focus on solving the ones that are most interesting to you. There are always more problems to solve than people to solve them, so aim for opportunities where you can solve the problems that interest you most.

Work in Your Zone of Genius

In *The Big Leap*, author Gay Hendricks advocates that we work in our "zones of genius"—things we do well that come naturally to us. Ideally, your zone of genius is at the intersection of what you're good at and what your company needs.

Every Day, Work Toward Personal Goals
Aligned with Greater Company Goals

Working at a startup can feel a bit like sailing upwind; a direct course is never possible, and the conditions can shift mightily along the way. Your goal as a startup employee is to understand the company goals, and then create mini goals and objectives for yourself that you'll work toward every day.

Software engineer and thought leader Patrick McKenzie says:

Approach your job as if you're creating case studies for your future self. Attach a measurable outcome to everything whenever possible. If you're a designer, keep design artifacts. When planning a project, get group consensus about what success looks like and signoff on sharing it on the company blog. Instead of showing up and trying not to get fired, actively collect case studies and create a bouquet out of them so you can have things to demonstrate. This will ensure you enjoy work more and are happier.

Each day, map out the two to three priorities that you ab-solutely want to achieve before the end of the day, ensuring that each of these are aligned with company priorities and objectives. Each week, ensure your overall goals are aligned in your one-on-ones with your manager. This will enable you to constantly ensure that your work is directly impacting the company's bottom line and objectives.

If you manage a team, ensure everyone is aligned with the overall goals of a project. It isn't your goal to micromanage each team member's individual work. However, you'll need to make sure that over time your team is achieving the goals you set out to achieve.

Figure Out the Tools and Systems That Work Best for You
You'll likely need to adapt to software and systems already in place at a startup, though depending on when you join and the role you have, you may have some freedom to help determine what systems are selected. Within the compa-ny-wide software platforms and tools, you should also have your own self-management systems; these may be a

combination of the official tools, some unofficial software, and even non-tech tools.

For example, your company may track work in Atlassian Jira (a project tracking tool), but for yourself, making a list of top action items and priorities in Evernote or a textedit file may be what you need to ensure you're staying on track with your priorities. Creating and adopting systems for your personal productivity used in conjunction with official external (meaning company-facing) tools is key to ensuring you're matching your personal goals with priorities. Make a list of the top priorities for the day, week, month, quarter, and/or financial year in whichever system(s), and do what you can to accomplish them to the best of your ability.

Remove Distractions Where Possible

When you start your workday, what is the first thing you do? Do you check emails, scan your company's internal communication system (if you're working at a startup, you're likely using Workplace by Facebook, Slack, or another communication platform), or check social media? How often do you feel distracted throughout the day, and by what? Some startup offices are more distracting than others. Whatever your situation—even if you work remotely—do your best to minimize distractions.

This is easier said than done, especially in startups with open offices. As you go through your priorities for the day, week, quarter, and financial year, and find that you're unable to complete them, you may need to adjust either your workload/expectations or your level of distraction throughout the day.

I enjoy setting aside time in the morning, before checking

any device, to just "be." That time may be spent writing in a journal, spending time with loved ones, or reading a book. I take care to limit distractions during the day, especially when I need to focus on a creative task. Open offices are challenging for me as an introvert, so I consciously balance in-office face time with time working remotely or from a quiet room in the office. Sometimes I overdo it and work too late at night or become burned out from too many meetings. Figuring out what works for yourself at work is an art, not a science. Be gentle with yourself if you become imbalanced. The idea is to notice when it happens early on so you can course correct before experiencing burnout.

Be a Learner and Adopt a Growth Mindset

Carol Dweck's book *Mindset* has made a big impression within Silicon Valley, and for good reason. Dweck's research shows that having a "learning" or "growth" versus a "fixed" mindset is crucial.[30]

Brian Balfour, CEO at Reforge, formerly VP Growth at HubSpot, EIR at Trinity Ventures, and founder of numerous other startups, suggests that career advancement requires figuring out how to solve new problems as they arise and employing an attitude of learning to adapt to changing market needs. He says:

> Becoming an elite professional has nothing to do with the specific hammer in your toolkit and everything to do with mastering the emerging skills, frameworks, and thought processes that enable you to solve new problems, repeatedly.[31]

Brian suggests that instead of focusing on being a "generalist" or a "specialist," it's crucial to focus on fundamentals, those core skills that are applicable as you begin to solve "harder problems." Brian also recommends choosing "growth projects," which he defines as projects that have "high organizational impact" and are unpopular with others in the organization.[32] He says these projects are "messy," put you at the center of attention, and teach you a lot.

CHAPTER SEVEN

MANAGING YOUR CAREER

Take Charge of Your Own Career

If you don't manage your career, no one else will. You'll marshall support and recruit mentors throughout your career, but ultimately you're the one who needs to oversee your own career trajectory.

Set Your Sights on What You Want

Do you want to be in the C-suite of a startup? Do you want to be promoted to oversee a large team, with the freedom and responsibility to set your own agenda and deliver outcomes? Would you like to be an individual contributor, preferring not to manage others and instead be rewarded for your expertise and results? Work with a friend, coach, or mentor to help identify what you'd like your career path to look like (it's totally OK—and to be expected—if this changes over time). You can work with your boss to create a plan to hit the targets you've set for yourself, and if you can't achieve your career goals within your company, it will become clear.

Find Your Role

An in-depth exploration of what each startup role entails is beyond the scope of this book. If you're not sure which startup role is right for you, Jeffrey Bussgang's fantastic book *Entering StartUpLand* is an incredible resource.

Kate Catlin, founder of Find My Flock, an engineering staffing company, says she often hears from engineers who want to transition to other roles but feel stymied because they are unsure what different roles actually entail and whether or not they'd enjoy them.

If you're considering a role you haven't held before, it's a great idea to connect with those who are already performing the role. Search for people with the job you're exploring through social media or through in-person networking and ask if they'd be willing to take a few minutes to get coffee or have a phone call to discuss what the role entails so you can get a better sense of whether it would be a fit for you.

Talk to a sales engineer to find out what they actually do (combine their technical knowledge of a product or service with explaining this to prospective buyers) *and* what their day-to-day work experience is like (demoing software to customers, sending emails, etc.). It is helpful to understand whether you'll be doing activities that you enjoy—or not.

Find Your Niche within Your Industry and Specialty

As much as you can, specialize. Can you be known for being an expert in a particular vertical or niche? When I specialized in B2B SaaS marketing for customer success-focused companies, my career took a leap. Additionally, when I took over our VOC program, no one wanted to touch it, but there was a big organizational need. I had to learn a lot to do it well. This led to me taking over our customer marketing program and becoming the go-to person for insights from our customer base for several of our key products. There was no open position that I applied for, no vacant role that I stepped in to fill; I realized the need and took it over. This led to my promotion. You can do this too.

Become Indispensable

Startups are constantly changing. Positioning yourself to become indispensable to multiple departments is a crucial way to keep going even in turbulent times. The key is thinking outside your department; question if what you're working on helps your startup's bottom line, whether you're writing lines of code or press releases.

A truly remarkable salesperson can't only be focused on her quota. Matt Harada has a great perspective on this:

> Does selling these two deals help the company in the long run? Are you hurting another department by selling the wrong deal? There may be things you could do to expand your role; if an accountant, you could become a controller. Think of how you can make your role bigger and of more use to more of the company to grow your influence.

Become a Thought Leader

Becoming a thought leader in your field is a great way to build your career. Ways to do this include:

- Co-hosting public-facing webinars for your company
- Blogging (in your own name)
- Stepping up to opportunities to speak publicly—local meetups are great places to start
- Posting about your startup niche on social media

Learn the Business Basics

If you didn't study business in school, fret not! Anything you can do to understand the broader business perspective will help you in your career. Books, online courses, and workshops can help you gain an understanding of business essentials, and you can work with a mentor to learn things such as how to read a profit and loss (P&L) statement, how to understand a function of the business you're not familiar with, and so on. No one knows everything in startups—not even (especially not!) the founder. Asking questions or doing research on your own will help you get a leg up and grow.

Managing Upwards: Hack Your Boss, Mentor, and CEO Relationships

Regularly Have One-On-Ones with Your Boss, and Always Create an Agenda

One-on-one meetings are the lifeblood of your relationship with your boss (and your direct reports). This is your chance to show your boss what you're working on, agree on how you're providing value to the company, surface any issues (immediately) and also get feedback on any areas where you're stuck. If your boss hasn't already set up a regular weekly one-on-one, ask to put a recurring meeting on the calendar.

Here are three tips for holding successful one-on-ones with your boss:

1. **Create an agenda.** In your agenda, you should cover each of the areas you work on. Even if you haven't made significant progress on a certain area that week, you should include it so your boss understands the scope of the work you're managing. Include significant progress in each area, noting what you've accomplished and any blockers. The goal will be for you to have a high-level discussion with your boss about what you've achieved that week, what you're planning to work on next, and any challenges you've encountered. This makes it easy for them to go to their boss or board and let them know what you're working on in each area. Advance awareness of blockers also positions them to help you get unblocked.

2. **Agree on short-term goals and priorities.** Each week when you meet with your manager, ask him or her to confirm that the goals and priorities you're working on are still relevant. At startups, things move fast. You want to ensure that what you're working on is still important, and weekly one-on-ones are the best way to check in about this. That way, no more than a week can go by with you working on something that is no longer a priority.

3. **Check in regularly about your long-term goals.** One-on-ones are your chance to discuss your long-term

goals, as well as how your boss can help you meet them. If there is something you want, your syncs with your boss are a good time to bring this up. This also sets a precedent when asking for raises and promotions.

Other Ways to Grow Your Career

Manage Up

Find out what is important to your boss each week and focus on those priorities. Don't be afraid to push back and let them know when they're wrong, but never be disrespectful. Don't be afraid to ask questions—everyone in tech is figuring it out. If you have questions, vocalize them. In the meantime, try to see the big picture. Know what's going on in other departments; look for strategic patterns across the company instead of being limited only to your department. Move projects forward, communicate, and keep everyone in the loop. Understand your boss' problems and deliver solutions. Be as easy to work with as possible, and do your best to enable your boss to be successful. In turn, your boss will be committed to helping you be successful.

Special Note: What to Do If Your Boss Isn't Happy at Your Startup

Your primary job at a startup is to advance the mission of the business. As part of that, it is important to ensure your manager is successful. Pay attention to your boss' happiness. If your boss isn't happy at work, it may be temporary—or they may be on the way out. It is important to keep in mind that we all go through phases where we are more or less happy in our roles; your boss may be going through a difficult time at home, or in the midst of a normal period of dissatisfaction or disengagement at work. If your boss is truly unhappy, you should take note. The best managers shield us from negativity upstream; sometimes we can't see or they aren't at liberty to talk about things that will come to impact us only in their absence. Is your boss noticing issues with their management that, if they leave, you will be left to face?

Your manager may be facing a change at home or just ready for a new opportunity. They may not tell you when they're ready to move on, but if you notice signs of increased frustration or disengagement, it can't hurt to ask. Even if they don't answer directly, there may be clues; do they seem more regularly irritated or blame things on "management" or "execs"? If they are an exec, do they blame the CEO or the board? This can mean there are deeper issues happening that they are unable to share with you but that may signal trouble ahead for them or for the company.

What to Do If Your Boss Is Leaving

You may choose to stay on if your boss leaves, or you may not; either way, get as much information as you can. It is important to understand why your boss is leaving. Investigate the reasons, if they are open to sharing with you. If you respect your boss deeply, and they're frustrated with aspects of the business that you're not aware of, be sure that once they leave, you'll need to deal with those issues. Often the managers we like are also our mentors, and they can give us access to the opportunities, projects, resources, and senior leadership that offer the greatest career growth. It may be harder to get this leverage without this person, though it may be worth sticking around to see if someone new is able to help you get what you need—or eventually you might be able to step into your boss' role.

At this point, it is wise to map out potential plans for how you'll handle the transition. Ideally you'll have built relationships with other departments so you could move to a new area if your boss leaves, and hopefully you'll have a sense of whether the issues your boss is experiencing are personal or a warning sign that it's time for you to move on too. If you aren't already exploring other opportunities, it's wise to apply to other companies to give you options in case your boss' replacement isn't someone with whom you'd like to work.

Consider options for potentially taking on your boss' role (and getting a promotion in compensation and title!). If you do decide to stay, follow all the steps outlined in this chapter to build rapport with your new manager. Embrace new leadership if you're staying and not taking your boss' spot, and do your best to ensure that person's success.

Remember: no matter what, if you have a great relationship with your manager, there is no reason why you can't stay in touch with this person after they move on. That's one of the best parts of startup life: collecting wonderful relationships along the way.

Find and Invest in Your Mentors

We often approach mentorship thinking about what we can gain from the relationship. Instead, it is helpful to think about how you can help those around you.

Build a Relationship with Your Startup's Founders and CEO

When you join the company, if not before, introduce yourself and form a personal connection. Get to know the founders as people—do their values truly align with the company values and your own? What do they do for fun outside of work? Most founders in Silicon Valley have conversation-worthy hobbies such as music or art or some intense physical sport. Many take these up to become better networked in the Valley, or to blow off steam.

Regardless of whatever they're interested in, you should take some time to learn about it. It's not sucking up; if you were married to someone or had a close friend interested in something, you'd want to learn more about their interests to better connect with them. It's no different with the founder of a startup. Do they love guitar and practice any chance they get? Ask them about their favorite artists and explore their catalogue. The key isn't to be fake; it's to genuinely try to find common ground through their interests.

You need to provide some unique value to the founder; is there a project they have always wanted accomplished that you can work on? Is there some specific pain they're having you can help solve? Try to be helpful to the founder, and you'll make it worth their time to invest in you.

Depending on the size of your company, access to the CEO may be harder to get, but make sure you have it, at least partially. Be aware that making inroads with a CEO isn't a substitute for having a good relationship with your manager. SendGrid co-founder and former CEO Jim Franklin says he could always tell when an employee was attempting to ingratiate themselves for ulterior motives:

As a former CEO, I really liked it when individual contributors would make an effort to reach out, but too often they were just hedging because they had already lost the support of their direct supervisor. So make sure that all is good with your direct supervisor and don't try to do an "end run."

Hiten Shah says that if you're working at a company with less than twenty-five people, the founder should be paying attention to *you*.

Shah says "it gets sketchy after twelve people," but once a startup grows to twenty-five people, it's harder for founders to maintain relationships with the entire team. At two hundred people, he says, usually founders realize they don't and can't know everyone.

Building and maintaining a relationship with your founder(s) can help you align with the company. At small startups, you may report directly to the CEO, at least at first. If you're at a larger company, make an effort to connect with the CEO as much as possible. Even at a 250-person startup, you can find time to do activities with the CEO, perhaps in smaller groups (for example, hiking with them or having a special team lunch that includes them). Staying connected to the CEO enables you to really align with their vision and also gives them a chance to get to know you and your work.

CHAPTER EIGHT

WORKING ON A TEAM

Just as you pay attention to your own productivity, be intentional about the way you work with a team. Teamwork is at the heart of startup life. Some of the best friendships of your life can come from team members. Startups are also stressful, so alternatively stress can erode relationships.

Take Responsibility for Your Team and Your Work

Whether you are the most junior person on your team or the team lead, each person needs to prioritize the success of the team over their own success. This is not to say that you can't own your hard work or be rewarded for it accordingly through raises and promotions. You will take credit as an individual by documenting your successes and sharing them each week in your one-on-ones.

It is crucial to use "we" language. Think "we shipped the new product" versus "I shipped the new product." Everything we do at a startup is a result of teamwork, and using inclusive "we" language shows that you are aware of this. Your colleagues will trust you more when they don't think you're always angling for credit. (Note: If a colleague consistently takes credit for your individual contributions, you have to call them on it. See the section later in this chapter discussing strategies for stopping and preventing this.)

Honor Your Colleagues' Wins

When your colleagues do amazing work, praise them for it. Some startups have formal systems for recognizing awesome behavior (many call it "kudos"). Make a habit of seeing and recognizing the outstanding work of your colleagues. They will return the favor.

Focus on Work Relationships as Well as the Work Itself

Relationships are the most crucial aspect of startup life. The people with whom you're working are in the same proverbial boat as you, and nothing in a startup can move forward without a team effort. Take time to get to know your colleagues on a personal level. Celebrate their work accomplishments and "wins." Learn about their interests, hobbies, families, and lifestyles. This journey is more fun when it is shared with other people.

Address Any issues You Have with Colleagues with the Colleagues Directly

As much as you can, stay out of office politics and gossip. When you have an issue with a colleague, you should bring it up with them directly. If you talk about someone else, only say things that you'd be willing to get back to them. There are exceptions to this, but as a general rule, if you have a problem with someone, always confront them directly.

WORKING ON A TEAM

If you are a manager, make it clear that you expect this of your team. Encourage your direct reports to bring up issues they have with one another directly; don't allow yourself to be the go-between. If necessary, facilitate a conflict resolution, but it's always best if your team can confront issues with each other directly.

Build Relationships with Others in Your Industry (See Your Industry as a Team)

It's important to network with others in your industry; these are the people who will refer you to their company for your next job (and vice versa) and help you on your career path. Networking can feel slimy; authentic relating never is. Aligning yourself with people who are passionate about things you are also passionate about is genuine and crucial.

Be Remarkably Helpful to Your Peer Network

You have to support your peers. In *Disrupt Yourself*, author Whitney Johnson says to focus on your strengths to make the biggest impact.

> What compliments do you shrug off? All too frequently, we are oblivious to our own strengths. The trouble with certain strengths is you do them so reflexively well they can be easy to overlook.[33]

Johnson advises we pay attention to the compliments we "habitually dismiss" because the "thing" comes so naturally to us. ServiceRocket COO Erin Rand describes this as finding our "superpower."

Rand says the secret is to find opportunities where we can work with people whose superpowers complement ours.

What to Do When Someone Takes Credit for Your Work

While you won't get credit for every single bit of work you do, especially when you're in management, it is absolutely essential that you receive acknowledgment for your important contributions to projects. Most of the time, when credit for your involvement is omitted, it's unintentional. Sometimes, though, it's not. Either way, set the precedent that when someone else takes credit for your work or neglects to mention your involvement on an important project, you'll speak up. If you don't, you'll harbor resentment and lose key recognition for your efforts. If someone other than your manager consistently takes credit for your work, you can confront them politely; if they make a habit of it, it's OK to say something publicly, such as "Thank you for expressing my idea, John. I'm glad you support it too."

CHAPTER NINE

AVOIDING BURNOUT

Burnout is an unfortunately common side effect of startup culture. It's important to take steps to mitigate burnout, both in yourself and in your teams.

What does burnout look like?

- Mental and/or physical exhaustion
- Intrusive thoughts about work interfering with the rest of your life
- Being frequently irritable, tired, or depressed

Startup Weekend founder, serial entrepreneur, and startup community builder Andrew Hyde says that he's seen many in the startup ecosystem become burned out.

> As an employee or founder, people don't think enough about what they need on a personal level. I think people get trapped in startup excitement, but they need to understand who they are and what matters most. If you don't know who you are and what your values are, joining a startup is a really bad idea.

According to Hyde, if you want to reserve a lot of time for family, joining an early-stage startup can be a "terrible idea." He says "You'll have zero time for your family, always traveling, stressed out and working. Identify where you want to be going over the course of your career and life."

Avoiding burnout requires conscious effort on your part, as well as making sure you work for a startup that enables you to take time to protect yourself against the negative effects of working too hard.

Pink Coconut founder and activist Donnya Piggott says:

In the Caribbean, we have a saying: "You can't pour from an empty cup." By taking care of you, you take care of the business. When we do our work we push ourselves hard because we care and want the work to get done, but there must be that balance. If there isn't and you keep pushing and you leave yourself out, it's no help to the business. It's important to practice self-care and acknowledge when to stop working. When you're burned out, everything suffers, and you can't do work. I had to learn this the hard way. The movement I want to build benefits from my rest and being an improved leader.

Thriving During Constant Change

Chaos is often the status quo at startups. That's not a bad thing; it makes sense. As companies grow, complexity is added before processes to manage this complexity are implemented. The people who do best at startups are those who can create value during times of ambiguity.

Some people naturally seek the status quo; they may not

feel the most comfortable at startups or larger technology companies. Generally speaking, the larger the company, the slower the rate of change. But if you want to make an impact, you need to become comfortable with constant change—without getting burned out.

Find Stability in Other Areas of Your Life
Figure out what activities relax and center you, whether that's spending time with family, being alone in nature, meditating, working out at the gym, shooting pool, reading books, going for walks with your dog, or racing motorcycles. Immersing yourself in something you enjoy on a regular basis will help you stay sane when work feels like it's constantly in flux.

Working Remotely

Many startups offer employees at least occasional remote work options, which can really help as you navigate having a life *and* having a startup career. Whether you're remote one day per quarter or one day per week, having the opportunity to work outside business hours from your own space can really help maintain balance.

I worked remotely for nearly eight years prior to joining my current company, and while assessing my current role before joining, it was important to me that the culture included some remote work. A full-scale guide to how to manage yourself and others while working remotely is beyond the scope of this book, but I've included some great resources in the *Recommended Reading* section at the end.

Work/Life Balance

A recent study found that flexible work environments made for happier, more productive employees.[34] Today's most innovative startups recognize that creating positive work environments yields better business results.

Many companies state clear policies addressing how they approach the subject of rest and vacation, as well as how likely you will be to find people working on the weekends. However, work/life balance most often varies by team, so you'll want to understand how your direct manager and peers behave before you join. Ask questions about how likely people are to take their PTO, how often your direct team members work weekends, work late at night, etc. It will be easier to ask these questions of peers rather than your direct boss, but do find out.

In *Killing It*, Sheryl O'Laughlin shares an important reminder that no matter our life situation, our boundaries and needs matter:

> If you're working with someone who doesn't have a
> significant other or kids, it's still equally important for them
> to take time for personal priorities. Sometimes parents
> think they're the only ones who have priorities. Assure your
> team that you understand the importance of their lives, no
> matter who or what is in them.[35]

Work/Life Balance at Early- versus Later-Stage Startups

Generally speaking, early-stage companies have less formal structures and less clearly defined hierarchies than more mature companies. However, what many early-stage startups lack in structure, benefits, competitive compensation, or so-called work/life balance (i.e., long hours to meet crazy dead-lines), they tend to make up for in equity grants, stock, and in-work flexibility. You may have to work long hours at an early stage company, but you'll likely have more control over where and when these long hours occur.

When teams are small, many early-stage companies are supportive of making work as flexible as possible. Early start-ups often offer employees increased control over their work environment, including flexible hours and the option to work remotely. Note: if you're working for an early-stage company that doesn't offer flexibility *and* comes with all of the hallmark grind features of early-stage companies, consider looking for work elsewhere.

As startups grow past the early stages—after they've suc-cessfully fundraised or, if they're self-funded, have experi-enced significant traction—their work environments tend to become less flexible. While choosing which companies to work for, ask about work/life integration. Specifically, ask for practical examples of how people can leave early or work from home in order to accommodate their lives.

Startup executive Colleen Blake notes that management and executive-level employees will *always* experience increased con-trol and flexibility when it comes to their work environment. This is why it's so important to be a top performer at a startup in order to be promoted and gain increased control over your schedule and your work environment.[36]

Work-Life Balance at Rapidly Scaling Companies
Upon scaling, startups change. When there are five or six

people in the office, it isn't as big of a deal if the whole team or some of the team works remotely several days per week. Once there are fifty people in the office, startups need to create rules and systems to manage everyone and everything. When startups are paying so much for office space, it makes sense to want people to show up to use it. Instead of conducting customer meetings off-site, they now come to your office, so suddenly it makes sense to ensure the office looks presentable, and now employees need to dress the part—especially if you have enterprise customers or customers outside the startup bubble (for instance, doctors visiting a health tech startup or lawyers stopping by a legal startup).

At fifty people, that open office may become filled with distracting noise and activity. The sales development team at a mid-level company may be making calls alongside the content marketing team, who need to focus on writing copy for ebooks, and may also be distracting the finance team, who need to ensure bookings and billings are on track.

In general, larger startups often have more HR infrastructure in place. They are more likely to offer great perks—those in-house gyms, nap pods, and coconut water—while mid-level startups may be still working out the kinks, so they may have some of these perks but sporadically offered, or they may not offer them at all.

That doesn't mean mid-level startups don't offer great work environments. In fact, many of the best work environments can be found at companies with twenty to 150 people in the office. Larger companies that have acquired smaller startups can often maintain the feel of smaller offices. Scaling startups may choose to have an open office environment for financial (or aesthetic) reasons as they grow. However, it's possible to create cloistered mini environments within the office for employees to work on more demanding tasks, or allow them to work at a coffee shop nearby or remotely several days per month as needed.

There isn't a one-size-fits-all approach to creating more balanced work environments. Try to work for a company that accommodates different personalities, styles, and needs in order increase the likelihood that you'll feel fulfilled, comfortable, and able to do your best work. If you manage a team, consider ways to offer flexibility to those in your charge. That will vary from team to team, from role to role.

A sales development representative (SDR) simply must be by the phones most of the time, but maybe you can remotely route calls to work occasionally. Perhaps you don't feel you can work remotely full-time; perhaps you could potentially work remotely at least a few days per month. Consider ways you can encourage balanced habits among your team. Take walking meetings rather than always gathering in a conference room, when the situation permits. These are obvious things, but we so easily forget them while we're caught up in the fray of growing startups.

Vacation

It can be hard to fully go off the grid at startups. Maybe you're of the mind that it's fine to work some weekends or check email while you're on vacation. Or, perhaps you'd rather not—ever—and don't want to be expected to. Either way, find out what the norm is among the people on your team and decide if it aligns with your preferred style. A note on companies that offer "unlimited vacation": At first it may seem as though you'll truly get unlimited time off, but in truth, people don't really take unlimited vacations—in some ways having a number of days or weeks to hit makes you more likely to take them. There can be guilt associated with taking vacations that have no limits.

To address this, BareMetrics' CEO Josh Pigford instituted a "minimum vacation" policy and took other steps to ensure employees actually took ample vacation time.[37] Startups like the concept of unlimited vacation because then they don't have to pay you for time off you don't take, whereas with set days, they do have to pay you. If you see an "unlimited vacation" policy, be sure to ask lots of hard-hitting questions about whether it is actually used. For instance, Netflix has an unlimited vacation policy but actively encourages employees to take long, unplugged breaks. Find out whether unlimited vacation leads to people actually taking significant time off.

Family: Flexible Time, Parental Leave, and More

The sad reality in America is that parental leave is not required; many startups claim to be—or maybe even want to be—family-friendly, but they have pretty rough policies when it actually comes to taking leave. As a parent, or future parent, what kind of flexibility can you expect? Look for a place that prioritizes outcomes over specific hours worked. Studies show that working parents do a damn good job of getting their work done and can be productive outside work hours.[38] If you need to be in the office at 11:00 a.m. in order to take your kids to the doctor that morning, but you're willing to work late at night from home to ensure projects are completed, an employer should respect and honor that as equally valid as the person who works a "typical" day. Many startups are recognizing the importance of parental leave and helping employees, especially women, come back to work when they are ready and on their own terms. This isn't an easy topic, but asking around can save you a lot of pain. There are places willing to honor your ability to both work and fulfill your role as a parent—if you can, don't settle for somewhere that makes you sacrifice.

Parental leave isn't just for women. In *Killing It*, Sheryl O'Laughlin explains that the industry needs to address this for everyone:

> [Men] may not feel as much judgement about missing their kids' activities as moms do (although some now do), but that doesn't mean they want to be working a zillion hours and missing first steps and doctor's appointments.[39]

A Word on Startup Business Travel

I remember my first international business trip to Santiago, Chile. I spent a month in my startup's office there, which involved spending time with colleagues and giving a talk at a local startup accelerator. I traveled with colleagues from our local US office, and I had a wonderful time with them and my Chilean colleagues, enjoying the pace of the local office culture (two-hour lunches!) and the opportunity to travel around Chile on the weekends. It was a lot of work with a lot of relaxing mixed in. In contrast, a recent international business trip I took to Australia and Malaysia just about wiped me out. The client work I was doing was much more intense than on my previous trip to Chile, and I also packed in more work in a shorter amount of time, halfway across the world.

The stress of my trip caught me by surprise; I had no idea, based on my previous trips, that traveling for work would be anything other than a fun experience. The point is that business trips can be fun and exciting—or draining and stressful. There are different time zones, foods, and customs to adjust to, client meetings in new locations, new colleague interactions, the stress of travel, and more. And many startups don't spring for business travel upgrades or other cushier accommodations that larger companies can afford. If you prepare yourself for an exhausting trip, you'll be more likely to do what you need to in order to stay balanced. Remember: business trips are not the same thing as vacations!

PART THREE

HANDLING TRANSITIONS

Startups change more quickly than most work environments, and the average job tenure is often shorter. Your experience at work can change pretty quickly. The chapters in this section cover how to deal with those changes.

CHAPTER TEN

SHOULD YOU STAY OR GO?

This chapter focuses on how to determine if you should stay at your startup, including the benefits of negotiating for a change, accepting your circumstances, or leaving. Things don't have to be terrible for you to want to leave your position at a startup; desiring new opportunities, a change in city or location, or even an entirely new role is very natural. People tend to shift roles in tech fairly frequently, so you're not alone if you're jonesing for a change.

That being said, there are plenty of reasons to stick it out long-term at a startup. If the company is doing well financially and you like the leadership team, you like other aspects of your job, *and* you can continue to advance your career through new responsibilities, raises, and promotions, staying is a great option. If you have equity, you may be rewarded financially by sticking it out. Here are a few things to take into consideration as you evaluate whether to continue working or move on.

Evaluating Your Options

People switch tech jobs frequently; it is a relatively accepted practice in Silicon Valley (and beyond). It is often easier to be promoted or get a significant raise at another company than your own. In addition, if there's something you don't like about your company, it can be very tempting to see if there is greener grass elsewhere. Most of us have days where we dislike aspects of our jobs. This is normal. If you get to the point where you discover that the negatives outweigh the positives, you have options: attempt a change, accept the circumstances (usually we do this temporarily), or work somewhere else. (Note: you should be constantly networking and lining up alternative options for yourself so you never feel stuck somewhere! You should stay because you want to.) If you're thinking about your options, here are some things to keep in mind.

Making a Change

If you aren't happy at your job anymore and you want a change, the first thing to do is to clarify what specific changes you'd like to see and then discuss it with your manager. If you've been at your startup for a while and feel that you have contributed significant value and deserve a raise or promotion that hasn't been given, claim that. Do your research in advance for what is standard for the market, and back up claims you make about your achievements with documentation. You should have been setting the stage for how your performance will translate to raises and promotions with your manager through your weekly one-on-ones for months or years, so this shouldn't be a surprise to them.

Sometimes our managers aren't in a position to give us a raise or promotion right away. Think about other things you could negotiate for that would increase your happiness at your company. Ideas include:

- Shift your responsibilities to something you're more interested in, or new "stretch projects" or responsibilities that will enable your growth
- More vacation days (if your company doesn't offer unlimited PTO already)
- Travel opportunities to a company HQ or client location that you're excited to spend time in
- A standing desk or other equipment that would make you feel more balanced at work
- Attendance at an industry conference you're interested in
- A health club membership, wellness stipend, or other benefits that may not already be included in your contract

Accepting Things as They Are

Sometimes, we can look around us and say, "I didn't get what I want right now, but I want to stay." People's reasons for staying in circumstances that don't feel ideal are myriad, but they may include financial reasons or the desire for stability, especially if your home life is currently less even-keeled. Perhaps you haven't totally bought in to the company's direction post-pivot (meaning they started out doing one thing, but changed course to do another thing, sometimes in an entirely new market), but you are willing to live with the ambiguity long enough to figure out whether you can be happy. In the meantime, whatever the situation, if you do stay, you'll need to accept circumstances for the time you're there. Otherwise you'll drive yourself up the wall with everything that isn't right, eventually your performance will lag, and you'll find yourself miserable. But if you really can't accept things . . .

Go Work Somewhere Else

Even if you like your current role and company, you should be consistently networking and looking for new opportunities. Ideally, if you've done this, you will have some options when you decide to leave. If you don't have something waiting in the wings, once you determine that you no longer want to stay at your company, apply for roles that look interesting and ask friends if they have any jobs you'd be interested in at their startups. (See the section on finding a job for more tips on this.)

If you are financially able, it doesn't hurt to take a little time off in between roles so you can head to your next job feeling refreshed. When you're ready to move on, you want to take the time you need to find the right next fit rather than hurry away from your current role without doing due diligence only to land somewhere with similar problems. Of course, there is no shame if you really have to make ends meet and run to something—anything—to get you out of a job you don't like or can't stand. When you're ready, you'll look again and eventually find something that makes you happier and more fulfilled *and* pays the bills.

Is It Time to Move on from Your Startup Job?

Within Silicon Valley, leaving a job after only a year or two isn't uncommon. Jim Franklin suggests it is actually crucial to leave if you want to continue learning.

"You learn so much more by getting into a new industry," says Franklin. "I think about every three to four years is the optimal tenure."

In the Valley, frequent job-switching may be even more exaggerated than in other industries. How should you decide when to move on from your startup job? Here are a few considerations to keep in mind.

Do You Still Align with the Mission, Values, and Product(s) of the Company?

Is the company working on projects and products you believe in? Do you believe in the company mission, values, and product(s)? Misalignment between the company's direction and mission and your personal values and interests should be cause for you to consider moving on.

Do You Still Believe in the Founder/CEO and Leadership Team?

If you've lost confidence in the company's leadership, it makes sense to strongly consider leaving. If your confidence wanes temporarily, that's normal, but if you no longer have faith in the decisions made by the leadership team and/or CEO, that's a problem. You're not doing yourself (or the company) any favors by staying somewhere long-term where you're misaligned.

Have You Been at the Company for Years without Being Promoted, Given a Raise Commensurate with the Value You're Bringing, or Gaining Equity?

If you're doing an extraordinary job, you should be rewarded for it. If you aren't, think carefully about whether this current company is meeting your needs. If you can't change your situation, there's no need to accept it!

Are the Reasons You Joined the Company the Reasons You're Staying?

Did you join the company to achieve an outcome? Perhaps you wanted to work for a certain boss, and that person left. Or you wanted to complete a project or learn a new skill, and that milestone has passed. Be honest about whether things have changed in a negative way.

Do You Align with the Company Values as They Are Lived at the Company?

Are you seeing unethical behavior or behavior that simply doesn't align with your personal values? It's time to move on.

Are You Still Learning?

Learning is the key to a startup career; if you're no longer learning, it's time to leave.

Are You Working within Your "Zone of Genius" in Your Role—at Least Some of the Time?

Gay Hendricks describes our "zone of genius" as the area of work we really enjoy and fulfills us on a deeper level. At startups, we often operate in our "zone of excellence" or "zone of competence" (and sometimes "zones of incompetence"). If you're not doing the work that makes you excited to come in every day, and it's been a while since you've felt that way, reevaluate whether something needs to shift in your role.

Researching What Your Position Is Worth in the
Market, Is It Clear That You Could Make a Lot More
in a Similar Role at Another Tech Company?

Are you being underpaid according to the market? Would a new job come with a big raise that could positively help you and your family? When it comes down to it, if your company is fifteen years old and has no IPO or exit strategy in sight, any stock options are probably going to stay pretty worthless. It's hard to pass up restricted stock units (RSUs) that represent real money at other companies.[40]

Is There Another Significant Financial Reason to Stay or Leave?

Would a move away from your company impact your ability to take advantage of equity at your current company, and is that something that you're concerned about? The financial reasons for staying and leaving can make decisions simple. Get clear on the numbers to help you decide.

Ready to Go? Leave Gracefully

If you're leaving a startup, it's important to do so gracefully. Give your manager and your team as much time as possible to adjust to your impending departure, and work hard to make the transition smooth. The startup ecosystem is small, and you want to leave on a positive note to keep your options for the future open. The more energy you put into leaving on a positive note, the more it will be returned.

CHAPTER ELEVEN

LEVELING UP WITHIN YOUR CURRENT ORGANIZATION

Wherever you are in your startup career, you may have picked up this book specifically to figure out how to level up through promotions, raises, and more.

Our issues with negotiation in many ways are culturally specific. In America, we don't negotiate nearly as much as other countries. In school, if you put your head down and met job requirements, you were likely to be rewarded. Even in the workforce, at larger organizations, if you follow a set path you are likely to be promoted—there's a sense that organizations will look after you.

Unfortunately, startups aren't like this. Many founders lack management experience. Moreover, many early- and even later-stage startups haven't figured out things such as career paths. Even those that have don't always have clear ways for you to achieve the outcomes you want, including working on projects that are meaningful to you, being promoted, getting raises, and more. There are a lot of reasons for this, but know that it translates to this: if you want something to change, you have to be the one to drive that change.

There are many great books that cover the ins and outs of negotiation. I highly recommend *Getting to Yes* and *Bargaining for Advantage* as great places to start. In this chapter we'll focus on how to approach negotiation for specific scenarios you'll undoubtedly face in your startup career.

Career Growth

Most startups don't have a formal professional development program path; you must negotiate on your own behalf for projects and opportunities that will propel your growth.

Amplio Digital founder and CEO Marshall Hayes advises startup employees to remember that professional development is possible at startups, but it requires significant initiative on your part. He says:

> No one will care more about your career than you. Don't rely on your manager to develop you, but actively participate in creating a program to help you develop.
>
> "Can I or my manager come up with a program to continually develop me professionally? Can I take on special projects to develop, and can I do it consistently, week after week, month after month?" Each week at our company, we write down what we're grateful for, the number one thing we need from our manager to help us, and something that will help us develop. What professional development resources will we consume in the coming week?

Startup Promotions: The Basics

In the startup world, things move fast; there is a sentiment that if you haven't been promoted within two years, you need to switch companies. A recent study highlighted in *Forbes* pointed out that employees that stay in companies longer than two years get paid 50 percent less.[41] This is because raises (even for top performers) are based on base salaries, and when you switch jobs, you can command a higher base.

Negotiating a Startup Compensation Package

Sovrn chief of staff Sarah Innocenzi advises startup employees to always negotiate.

"You get 0 percent of what you don't ask for," says Sarah. "I always negotiate. I have more respect for people who negotiate than people who take the offer on the first go-around."

GutCheck Vice President of People Operations Josh Ashton says you should think critically about your personal risk profile when considering offers. A risk profile refers to your personal ability and willingness to take on risk. This includes the opportunity to get in on upside (forecasted increase in value) and reward in the case of startup exit or IPO with the chance of little to no windfall versus having the stability of cash in your income.

"Typically, if you're going to join a startup, you're going to have more upside on equity than you may have on cash," says Ashton. "It seems apparent, but during the offer process, people may understand that that's the situation but don't quite understand equity and options and percentages of ownership and dilution."

Determining Your Risk Tolerance

Determining your risk tolerance involves making an assessment of your own ability and willingness to take on risk in the form of variability and volatility. Google "risk tolerance" for some calculators to help you make an assessment. It's important to educate yourself on the company's current situation concerning their option pool and financing and their goals.

At this point, let's assume you like the title and other terms of an offer (office location, perks, vacation, benefits). Note: If you *aren't* happy with any of these things, you can bring them up during negotiation. In addition to the aforementioned, your offer will include cash and (hopefully) equity. Once you've determined how much risk you're willing and able to take on, you need to decide what matters most to you. Would you prefer to have more equity (and risk) or cash?

Social media platform Buffer, for instance, lets employees choose whether they want more equity or cash in their offer.

Your level of seniority in a company will determine how much equity you're entitled to. A VP will receive more equity than an entry-level role. The idea behind this is that the more senior you are, the more you are contributing and entitled to upside. That being said, if you join early enough, you may get significant equity. It must be emphasized: none of this equity may ever be worth anything, but it also could be worth a lot. This is why offers with equity components always carry more risk than cash, and they should be negotiated with reference to your personal risk profile. When joining an early-stage startup, the cash component will be lower than at a larger company.

"Cash is not why you're joining an early-stage company, and you should temper your expectations," says Ashton.

Ashton advises that if you're joining a small company or startup, you have to have a high risk tolerance and be willing to accept volatility in your offer in the form of equity.

"Once your startup's revenue looks good and stable and is predictable, then you can negotiate your original offer with the value you've brought to the organization," says Ashton. "I'd be hesitant to do too much on the front end; companies aren't often in positions where they can pay top of market from a cash standpoint. I'd wait to negotiate on the cash component when things are more predictable and heading in the right direction."

Ashton also says to remember that you're joining the company to create value, and that most of that value will be returned through equity if you've joined early enough.

"When you get to a place where the company is in a less volatile position, you're in a better spot to talk about and negotiate further," he says.

Cash versus Equity Offers at Early-Stage and Mature Startups

The breakdown of equity versus cash varies at early-stage and mature companies. More equity and stake in an eventual windfall, if it occurs, is a motivator for joining an earlier-stage startup. If you join later on, you may see a lot less equity or equity that is already diluted. Equity equates to ownership in the company. A startup that lacks the cash resources to pay market rate for our talents provides equity as an incentive for us to join, with the understanding that if the company succeeds wildly thanks to our help, we will have a piece of that success. Equity is our chance to get "skin in the game" and tie the company's success to our own. Of course, a startup may fail and your stock may be worth nothing. For someone new to startups, being offered 10,000 shares sounds amazing. You might accept a lower base compensation (annual salary) in exchange, not knowing how tricky that terrain is. Let's break down some of the common elements in the equity equation.

What Is a Share?

OptionValue.io defines a share as follows:

> A share of stock is a unit of ownership in that company.
> In public companies like Google and Apple, you can buy
> and sell this stock on exchanges. For private companies,
> it's more complicated, but you generally have to wait for
> a "liquidity event," such as the company going public or
> being acquired, before you can sell.

What Is a Stock Option?

A stock option is your right to buy the stock at a future date, usually after a vesting period. For example, I joined ServiceRocket in 2015, and each year I received new grants of stock options. I recently exercised some of my options that had vested by 2018. It took three years for most of these stock options to vest fully, and as of this writing, I still have additional stock options that were granted later that have not fully vested. I now hold a few certificates indicating that I own the stock; before, I just had the right to buy. When I exercised my right to buy some of my stock granted in 2015, it was at one price-per-share, and a different price for the options granted later. This is because of something called "strike price"; the price is set for how much each share will cost when the options are granted.

An option means you have the opportunity to purchase a share for a fixed price. Depending on how valuable the shares are, and what the fixed price is, options can be quite valuable. Imagine that you had the chance to buy tickets to the next Superbowl for twenty dollars each, for example. You could later resell them for a lot more than twenty dollars and pocket the difference.

What Is a Restricted Stock Unit (RSU)?

Charles Schwab defines an RSU this way:

> Restricted stock units (RSUs) are a way your employer can grant you company shares.
> - RSUs are nearly always worth something, even if the stock price drops dramatically.
> - RSUs must vest before you can receive the underlying shares. Job termination usually stops vesting.[42]

Josh Ashton says candidates should make an effort to understand how much equity is reasonable given the stage at which they join a company.

> There were people that joined SendGrid when we had three- to four-hundred employees and were Series D, but they were looking to join for the upside. We had to set expectations that it was far less about upside at that point. We took steps to educate them on what our option pool looked like and the percentage they'd receive, but in most cases, it was less than people were looking for.

When joining a smaller startup, you can expect more equity for the same role.

"If you have offers to join a five- to thirty-person company or a three-hundred-person company, both are small businesses, but your expectations shouldn't be the same in terms of options and equity ownership. It's a matter of educating yourself on what's common with equity and at various levels," says Ashton.

How Much Equity Is Appropriate for the Startup Stage I'm Joining?

A lot of smaller startups don't have the internal resources to understand what they should be paying people and what percentage of equity is appropriate. Ashton says that job seekers shouldn't rely on startups, and instead should take it upon themselves to gather the data they need by doing online research and asking people at other startups in the area how much equity they've received.

My advice for job seekers is to do a lot of research themselves. Come to the table with a lot of that data. This isn't a negotiation tactic; in turn you can talk it through with said startup; the startup and founders may benefit from that data. There's not a rich dataset of startup cash comp and equity comp comparisons. It's pretty organic. Ask the neighborhood what they're paying people. Smaller companies haven't paid for compensation consultants and databases. As a job seeker and candidate at the offer stage, don't be surprised that you'll need to do more of the research and information than the employer will.

It is crucial to understand your equity before accepting an offer. Whether you have multiple offers on the table and you want a better sense of what's happening, or you have one offer and want to understand the true value of what you're being offered, use online tools from reputable sites like Carta and OptionValue.io to gain the full picture.

A Final Word on Equity

Early startup employees can and do suddenly become millionaires after liquidity events, but it is, as founder and former SendGrid CEO Jim Franklin says, "exceedingly rare."

Josh Ashton cautions against being overly optimistic that this scenario will happen to you.

> I think people feel they'll join a startup because there'll be a windfall down the road through some sort of event, so that they'll be a millionaire in three to five years. They just have to work really hard and it will pay off in the long run. If you're joining the company and you are employee thirty, forty, or fifty, you'll be in a good position if the company is a built-to-last company. My former general counsel at SendGrid said that if you want to have this windfall opportunity or feel like you're going to be a millionaire by joining a startup, you need to be a founder. That's probably your best shot of seeing that come to fruition, even with odds being where they are. When we were fifty to one hundred people, people were joining who expected that would happen, and that was our advice to them. If you want the potential to be a millionaire down the road, then found a company that's successful.

Negotiation Tips

Many of us are brought up not learning how to negotiate. In the startup world, negotiation is a crucial skill that will serve you well throughout your career. Here are a few tips for negotiating successfully during scenarios you're bound to routinely encounter.

Negotiating a General Request

General requests might include asking for permission and funds to attend an industry conference or something else you want, most often from a manager but sometimes from a colleague. In this case, you want to outline what you need and why you need it. Make it easy for the person to say yes.

Write down specifics with dates attached to ensure that if you meet certain goals or criteria within a certain time, what you are asking for will be fulfilled. For example, if you meet your revenue targets, you will be sent to the top account-based marketing conference that spring in Hawaii. Make it specific, and get your boss to sign off on it. The key is to get this buy-in as far in advance as possible.

Negotiating a Raise

There is no one-size-fits-all rule about how often you should ask for a raise.

At smaller startups, promotions are often decided by the CEO or founder. Even if your department lead is the one advocating for your promotion, at companies of a certain size, it's the founder who does the promoting.

So build your case. Work with your manager to outline the reasons why you deserve the raise, including market data and clear evidence that your efforts are yielding a high ROI.

Negotiating a Promotion or New Role

One of the most important skills a startup employee can learn is how to successfully negotiate promotions. In his book *Bargaining for Advantage*, author G. Richard Shell points out that during negotiation processes, our gut instincts often fail us.[43] We each have different innate bargaining styles, says Shell, and in order to become the best negotiators possible, we need to understand our own strengths and weaknesses, how to build trust, improve leverage, and more. In fact, trusting our intuition and instincts can be a serious hindrance when it comes to successful negotiation.

Internal promotions can be hard at startups. This is because many of us are wearing multiple hats at once. When does your new role officially start? This is where negotiation comes in. It's up to you to prove that the work you're doing or going to be doing warrants a new title and commensurate bump in compensation. Where you can, bring in data; this is the best tool for advocating for yourself. Have you been managing more people? Have you exceeded goals and expectations for your work? Have you demonstrated leadership in the market, such as speaking at industry conferences and events? Anywhere you can bring in relevant metrics strengthens your case.

How to Get Promoted

Usually people assume they'll be promoted through one of two paths: either a promotion will be handed down to them magically as gratitude for their incredible service, or they'll need to engage in a heated dialog with their boss, palms sweaty, mumbling some rehearsed lines about being a loyal employee and deserving a raise, and then hope and pray this will somehow turn into their boss giving them a promotion. Unfortunately, this is not how startup promotions work. To get promoted at a tech company, you'll need to set the stage for your promotion long before any face-to-face conversation takes place.

To get a promotion, do all of the things described in previous chapters about being an extraordinary performer. Work for a company that values your contributions. To show how they value you, they'll promote you—but most likely, you're going to have to ask for it. Here's the right way to set yourself up for a promotion.

Step 1: Plant the Seeds. Talk to your manager (who may be the CEO or founder, depending on how large your company is) and let them know that you want to be an extraordinary performer. You're not just looking to do what's in your job description (if you were lucky enough to get one); you're in this to win and do the best job possible. That's how you get promoted. You'll want to identify the key metrics on which your boss is evaluating you as soon as you can. Get them to agree that these are their key metrics.

After your conversation, you should send an email to your boss to confirm that the metrics on which you're being evaluated within the next three to six months are indeed the ones you heard and wrote down. Discuss what achieving them will yield in a reward, and how you envision the next stage in the company looking for you. If you're a junior-level marketer, maybe that next step would be moving into a manager role and hiring someone to help you now that you've mastered specific skills.

Step 2: Over-Deliver. This part isn't easy—but you can do it. You need to over-deliver on each of those metrics you discussed with your boss.

Step 3: Check in. After achieving in each of the areas

you've delivered and three to six months have gone by, check in with your boss about your reward. Important: the raise or promotion you're asking for may lag three to six months after this conversation.

At this point, your boss has everything needed to promote you. If it doesn't happen at this point, strongly consider moving on.

CHAPTER TWELVE

FINDING YOUR NEXT STARTUP JOB

If you want to work at another startup, here is advice on finding your next opportunity.

Make It Personal

It is always better to have a personal connection when applying for a role. Research companies you'd love to work for. If you know of anyone in your network whose job you admire, offer to take them out to coffee or schedule a phone call to learn more. Employees are often monetarily incentivized to refer people, but either way, a friend or acquaintance may be able to put in a good word for you. Referrals are a big deal; most startups offer some kind of bonus for employees who help recruit, so any friends you have at awesome companies are probably extra-incentivized to bring you aboard if they're happy and think you'd be a great fit.

Job Sites and Job Site Aggregators

The internet is an obvious source for startup jobs, including job posting sites such as Indeed, Monster, Glassdoor, and Ziprecruiter. You can also check out company websites for companies you'd be thrilled to work for to see if they have roles available in your area. If they don't, you can still be in touch.

Social Media

Increasingly, social media is a viable option for finding job openings. Company-owned profiles on LinkedIn, Twitter, Facebook, and other social networks may or may not be up-to-date, but it's worth taking a look.

Word of Mouth

Many job opportunities are advertised through meetups, conferences, and events. As you grow your startup career, you'll make more connections with people who can alert you to open positions that may be a fit. Let people know you're looking for opportunities, either publicly if you're currently between roles or privately if you're still at another company and need to be discreet. Be sure to tell your network about opportunities at your company to return the favor. Many startups incentivize their employees to bring in referrals.

Cold Reach-Out

The startup world is built on relationships, so if you have any that may help, leverage those. If you don't know anyone at a particular company, you can still get a leg up from the slush pile of random resumes. If you dig into a company's careers page and don't see a position available in your area of expertise, you can inquire. Your email should sound something like this:

I think company A is doing amazing things in the B space, and I would be thrilled to explore the opportunity to join the team and help in advancing the mission to become the best at C. I see you haven't listed any open positions in D right now; however, I hope you'll keep me in mind when the need to hire someone in this area arises. I would be able to provide value in these ways, and attached is my CV for reference.

A cold reach-out isn't as likely to pan out as warmer reach-outs, so if you have any connections, those can make a big difference.

Start Out as a Consultant

Sometimes tech companies will hire you first as a consultant, which is an excellent way to learn more about the company, determine whether you'd enjoy working there with a particular team, and decide how you'd be able to contribute value. Many companies post contract roles that can eventually evolve into full-time roles (though not always).

Additionally, many companies advertising full-time roles will let you join as a consultant first. The consultant-to-full-time model is a way to reduce risk on both sides, and frankly, more startups should be doing it. After a consulting project, if you realize that you aren't aligned for whatever reason, you've been paid for contributing, the company hasn't wasted time and energy fully onboarding you, and you're both free to move on to better fits.

To find consulting opportunities at startups that will segue into full-time employment, you can search job sites for contractor roles. It's not foolproof, but these can sometimes turn into full-time gigs. Inquire in advance whether that may be a possibility. Alternatively, if you're actively exploring a full-time role with a startup, ask if you can do a trial project together on a consulting basis prior to joining. Evaluating startup fit by doing actual work with a team is incomparable to any other method. It removes the guesswork of knowing whether the opportunity and team are as much of a fit as they initially seem to be, and it can save you a lot of pain down the line.

Getting Recruited

As your career progresses, recruiters will increasingly find you. Even if you're happy in your current role, it's never a bad idea to chat with the recruiters. It's a good way to ensure you have options and find out what your true market value is—which can be especially helpful if you've been searching for a while.

Joining a Bootcamp

Bootcamps are a great way to get into a programming career if you are motivated but lack the skills. Reputable programs boast a 95 percent success rate if you follow their career services guidelines; once you land a job as a junior developer, you will be able to continue to grow as a software developer throughout your career. But bootcamps aren't right for everyone. To understand who should join a bootcamp and how they should approach the task of finding the right one, Flatiron School's Head of Online Instruction Peter Bell shared advice from years spent helping people make these very decisions.

Here are the questions Bell recommends asking yourself before taking the leap.

What are your objectives?

Are you looking to get a full-time job as software developer, enhance your skills with front-end developer as a designer, or build the skills required to found a company? Each objective drives a different learning environment. Bell says the first job out of a bootcamp is the hardest job you'll ever get; after that, you'll be turning down offers within two years. Once you snag that first job, the only reason you won't succeed long-term is if you choose not to because you don't like the job.

Are you sure you need to participate in a
bootcamp to meet your career goals?

Bell says if you just want to be a product manager, you don't necessarily need to learn to code to manage developers. Learning to code gives you deeper empathy, says Bell, but if your only goal is to manage development, taking a bootcamp isn't the most effective way to build skills you need. In addition to focusing deeply on skills you don't need, bootcamps don't cover a lot of skills regarding product design, agile, kanban, scrum, workflows, and other important things. Bell says bootcamps are primarily training you to be a junior engineer, not to build or manage a development team. So make sure you really want software development skills or want to become a software developer.

Have you tried free online labs to see if you
actually like software development?

Bell recommends exploring Code Academy or Flatiron School's Bootcamp Prep Program, both of which offer labs for free. These free online programs will show you whether you enjoy the process. He explains:

The actual task of being a software developer is writing code. If it doesn't work, then you spend the rest of the minute, hour, day or week getting it to work. In general do you find that to be frustrating or an enjoyable challenge?

Bell says if you enjoy this process the way you enjoy doing crossword puzzles, great.

"If you get frustrated when tech doesn't work like it should, you won't enjoy the task no matter how much you like developer salaries and opportunities," says Bell.

Researching Bootcamps

Assuming you want to become a software developer or have another reason to attend a bootcamp, check out coursereport. com, where graduates provide feedback on their experiences. Bell advises that you take the time to look through those reports. Does a particular bootcamp align with your values and learning style?

Online versus In-Person Options

The first decision you'll need to make is whether you are going to do an in-person bootcamp or take an online course. Bell says the benefits of an in-person course is that it has much more structure.

"You complete the course in less time and build good friendships and connections that help you get through the program and succeed in your career over time," says Bell. It's easier to build a network during an in-person course.

"In-person is a wonderful experience," Bell says. However, if you live too far away, can't relocate, or have a job or family that make a sixty- to seventy-hour week impractical, there are a number of online programs.

Whether the bootcamp you're considering is in-person or online, Bell advises speaking with one of the instructors. It is important to understand the instructor's objectives and background. Bell advises interviewing a bootcamp company the same way you'd interview a prospective employer. He also says not to discount cultural alignment.

"You're looking for a place that values similar things," says Bell.

Ask specific questions about the learning environment. What do they do when students are struggling or having trouble with motivation or other issues? Admit your weaknesses up-front to see if it's a good fit for you. Bell says you'll get a good sense of whether the program adopts a "be tough or else you won't make it" approach or has a more supportive and engaging environment.

What's the Bootcamp's History?

It is not wrong for a bootcamp to be large, but there are cultural challenges with scaling in any organization. As with any company growing too fast, be particularly careful about the quality of the instructors you'll be working with, as this will have a big impact on your experience.

Bell advises asking for the bootcamp's jobs report. Ask for statistics on what percentage of grads get a job and their average salary, ideally listed by a third party. Those statistics can shed light on the quality of the program, regardless of scale.

Bootcamps aren't for everyone. Be clear about what you're

looking to achieve from attending one, whether it's the right program for you, and plan to invest energy into going above and beyond the requirements.

CHAPTER THIRTEEN

TOUGH TIMES: WHEN A STARTUP FAILS OR FLOUNDERS

Unfortunately, startup failure is more common than startup success. It is in everyone's best interest to get realistic about startup risk. You may pour the best years of your life into a tech company, and it won't succeed—or it may succeed, but without you, for many, many reasons. That doesn't mean your time will be for naught, but it's important to understand the risks involved and be aware of what can happen so you're not caught totally off guard. That will help you make decisions about what's right for you.

Startups Are Risky, Things Often Go Wrong, and Failure Is Likely

Startups are inherently risky. Most startups, even successful ones, are constantly fighting against failure. Building startups is *hard*, and even the best-run companies are beholden to unforeseeable market forces and luck. No matter the stage or funding status of a company, many startups regularly fight for survival. Even if things are seemingly going "fine," failure may be on the horizon, which is why startups are especially volatile and difficult for many.

There are different types of bad. There's "dysfunctional" bad, where there is a poor values-alignment fit with who you are. This looks like corruption, employee issues, and so on. A company may have a terrible culture but still be doing well in the market.

Then there is market performance bad. You could have the nicest, most competent team members and a great work environment, and the company could still fall flat on its face.

Startup failure usually happens over time, with the issues beginning far earlier than you can detect.

When Startups Fail

Matt Hessler was formerly Director of Search at Trada, a VC-funded company that was on an impressive growth trajectory. Trada was a darling of the tech press when it was founded in 2008 through most of its six-year tenure, regularly featured as one of the fastest-growing, most promising tech companies at the time. Trada raised nearly $13M in funding from investors over six rounds before famously shuttering in 2015.

Hessler says that, as employees, we tend to digest startup failure differently than founders. "If you're not the founder, you don't say, 'I failed'; you can see other places where people had ultimate decision-making authority and chose the wrong thing."

He says it's important to take stock of the company's failures in order to take that understanding to one's next job. Ask yourself, "Where were mistakes made?" and think critically about whether you missed any warning signs. When startups go under, Hessler says, it can be a cause for grief, and too often, employees don't take the necessary time to grieve. He explains:

As employees, we often have less personal grief than founders, but when you contribute in a meaningful way, you feel a strong level of malaise when it doesn't succeed, because you helped to create some of the things that pushed the business forward.

Hessler suggests giving ourselves permission to grieve when startups go under.

Give yourself a grieving process time. That burden is not a founder's alone. How deeply you feel that burden depends on the size of the team, but if you're one of those "in the garage," so to speak, when the business is starting, even if you're not the head person, you feel the same feelings.

Hessler advises that we give ourselves time not only to grieve emotionally but also see it as an opportunity to look critically at the business—from what went well to what didn't.

Hessler suggests asking ourselves during a failure event:

- Were there red flags you missed?
- Was there a lesson in the particular way the startup failed?

When Trada failed, Hessler reflected on the lessons he learned. Her noted that once venture capital poured into the business, an overemphasis on customer acquisition without enough retention systems in place caused the problems that led to Trada's failure.

We got put through the VC cheerleading. There was a definitive time where we took our $8.5M Series-B round. Google Ventures came in to speak to our management team, and we were told, "This is the time to get on the gas and think like a 500M company and hire like a 500M company." That attitude is different from a bootstrapped business where it's incremental and moving more methodically.

When you're handed a big investment check, your biggest challenge as a startup is choosing the right thing to do next. You'll have ten priorities, and you need to pick one thing. We made some wrong choices at Trada. We really hit sales and acquisition super hard with those resources and acquired a ton of new customers, but we had a very leaky bucket and weren't generating the appropriate amount of lifetime value from those customers to make acquisition cost worth it.

Our wrong choice was to hire a forty-person sales team and pay whatever and do whatever to bring in new customers. That gives you the up-and-to-the-right hockey stick of growth to see new customers added to the platform, but they didn't stay long enough to generate enough revenue. To what end are you driving new customers to the business that aren't profitable acquisitions? You'd never make that mistake in a bootstrapped business because you know the lights won't turn on next month if you don't generate customer revenue. Every business decision has to be challenged by a ROI conversation.

Hessler has brought the lessons from Trada with him as a leader at Vinyl Me Please, a music startup. "[At Vinyl Me Please] we can't just go into our huge venture bucket and have a higher burn rate this month. Each effort is essential. It brings a higher level of focus," he says.

What If Things Are Worse Than They Seem?

Impending startup failure isn't always obvious to the eye. Trada was a darling of the local tech industry in Boulder. Since its founding in 2008, Trada raised millions of dollars from A-list investors, including Google Ventures and Foundry Group, and had a prime location on Boulder's Pearl Street. Trada served company lunches and paid healthy salaries, and razor scooters littered the office. But its business plan proved unsound. It hired an army of sales executives to sell an enterprise solution, but its margins weren't stable; it had a churn problem, and all of the customer acquisition cost weighed against the cost of running the business became untenable.

Trada became unprofitable and needed to cut the fat. It went through layoffs and restructured from a staff of more than one hundred to under a dozen. The company downsized from its posh Pearl Street office and moved into a tiny shared office space several blocks away. I know all of this because, at that time, I was brought in as a marketing consultant to help the company.

Trada reworked their product to empower a self-service model, reducing the cost to acquire new customers, but ultimately they were unsuccessful and shuttered mere months after the last razor scooter tread marks had been made.

Like all startups, Trada put up a shiny facade to make

themselves look better to customers, investors, and the employees they were trying to recruit. After all, no startup is ever going to get the chance to be successful if it leads its sales pitch with its out-of-cash date. Before you devote your passion and time to a business that you heard was the hot new thing, make sure you look past the press releases about funding rounds and learn about the real challenges facing the business.

Don't confuse a hip, cool working environment with business success. Ask your hiring manager: "What are the things that could kill the company, and how is the business addressing those things?" If they just repeat the external marketing mantra, don't accept this answer. It may be a bad sign if the company isn't willing to return the trust they are asking you to place in them.

In *The Start-Up of You*, authors Reid Hoffman and Ben Casnocha suggest looking outside of one's company to fully understand how things are really going at a startup:

> For thorny, big-picture anxieties, it's sometimes hard to articulate specific questions to ask. Maybe something doesn't feel right at my job. What's going on? Ask your network.[44]

Reframing Failure

All startups face obstacles and risk failure. At Trada, business challenges were not hidden from employees. We talked openly about burn rates and cash in the bank. While Trada didn't successfully "exit," it was a success by other measures.

How do you know if the business challenges should be a deal breaker or whether you should take a chance on a longshot, as I did with Trada?

Former Trada CEO Matt Harada suggests that as we navigate our careers, we focus on what we can control: the people with whom we are working and the problems we will be solving. That way, even if the business fails, we still win. He says:

> The lesson I take away (from Trada) is to know why you're doing a startup. If you are trying to get rich and win the lottery by getting options in the next Google, you are going to be disappointed ninety-nine times out of one hundred. Even if all the press is favorable, there is just no escaping those odds, so to me that is a lousy reason to join a startup, and you'll likely be unhappy. You'll have to work in a crappy warehouse and take a pay cut and have two to ten times more work in front of you than going somewhere established. But if you like working with smart and dedicated people who believe in their mission and are brilliant and care about what they are building, then all of that stuff is worth it. And the winning-the-lottery aspect is just icing on the cake. It shouldn't be about trying to predict whether your startup is a unicorn. It should be about loving what you're doing and the people you're doing it with. On that score, (Trada) was a massive success to me.

Moving On from Failure

Failure is often glamorized among founder communities, but what about for employees? There can be a stigma around having worked for a failure. After all, don't we all want to be able to talk about our successes?

If you have worked for a failed tech company, the important part is learning from the company's failures and figuring out how to reframe the situation into lessons learned. Matt Hessler says being part of a failing startup can be an incredible learning experience and can help you avoid making the same mistakes at at another company. After a failure, former bosses or even VCs at a failed company often will help you find your next gig, and many will respect that you can move past the failure and not repeat whatever caused it at the next company.

CHAPTER FOURTEEN

YOU'VE BEEN ACQUIRED— NOW WHAT?

Imagine that you're working for a fifteen-person startup known for its tight-knit, values-driven, outdoorsy culture, and then suddenly, one day you're pulled into an all-hands meeting letting you know that your company has just been acquired by a big company headquartered across the country. You may know a little or a lot about this company, but either way, very soon, you will become their employee.

Acquisitions come with a high number of unknowns and are almost always a nerve-racking experience. Some questions that may arise:

- What will change, and will any of it markedly affect my work experience?
- Will the parent (acquiring) company share the same values as my current startup?
- Will my job become redundant or will I no longer be needed?
- More immediately, what will happen to

my PTO and benefits—will my spouse still
be covered on my health insurance?

In every acquisition you should be prepared for negative outcomes, but there are potentially very positive outcomes as well. Don't let fear overshadow the opportunities.

For instance, you could get a promotion, or perhaps you had equity that you could turn into cash during the acquisition, or there may be an opportunity for you to leverage the value you bring to the transition to negotiate a nice windfall. Acquisitions and their resulting transitions tend to be highly emotional, but there are ways you can empower yourself to make the most of an acquisition.

In 2015 Analiese Brown was the HR manager at the time of acquisition of ShipCompliant, then an approximately forty-person SaaS company in Boulder, Colorado. During the acquisition, Brown's role involved helping ShipCompliant through the transition, managing everything from the details of HR to helping employees grapple with the emotional elements of an acquisition.

Brown advises the following during an acquisition:

1. **Upon learning of an imminent acquisition, take it upon yourself to learn as much as you can.** Analiese determined that the key to successfully navigating a startup acquisition as an employee is to focus on how you can reframe it from something happening "to" you, to something you have the power to shape to better your future. Gathering information and learning helps you do this.

2. While there will be a lot that you don't know and can't know right away, **obtain as much information as you can about the acquiring company.** Research the acquiring company's:

- Leadership
- Financials
- Key customers
- Stakeholders

Search for recent press releases about them and check fundraising information websites such as Crunchbase and Angellist to determine whether they've fundraised and/or if they plan to go public one day. Try to find out what happened when they bought another company; did the founders stay, and if so, for how long? How many employees stayed? Some of this information won't be readily available, but you'd be surprised what you can dig up with some modern sleuthing.

You can learn from internal resources too. There might be a designated go-to person at your company who can answer your questions. This may be the CEO of your company, one of the founders, or the person managing HR or Finance.

You won't be able to find answers to all your questions, and some information will likely be private. The point isn't to compile a database of information; your goal is to take an active role in what's happening.

3. **For as long as you're planning on staying, commit to doing an outstanding job.** Don't let the shifting sands

environment of an acquisition be an excuse not to be a stellar performer. You need to put in extra effort during this period because whether you stay or leave, you will have people to impress either at the acquiring company or in a new role very soon. In many cases, you'll benefit from staying long enough to fully explore the opportunities present in an acquisition.

4. **Empower yourself by becoming actively involved in the transition.** Your company may form a group of employees who are interested in shaping the transition. If there are ways to get involved, you'll have access to information and will be in a place to shape the transition process.

    Every acquisition and integration is structured differently. The more you can be actively involved, the better the chance you'll feel positively about the outcome.

    Sam Altman, a partner at Y Combinator (a company that provides seed funding for startups), recommends adopting the mindset of "bridge builder." He says, "You don't want two warring factions. You want the new company to support you, and you want people to like each other." He advises making it your personal business to develop strong relationships with as many people as you can at the acquiring company and be a bridge as tensions inevitably rise.[45]

5. **Give up trying to keep things the same.** Things will change. That's a given. The only thing you can control is what you do about the changes.

    Take time to mourn or celebrate the startup

experience you had, and then roll up your sleeves, learn, and decide whether you want to stay or if you would be better off somewhere else. Sam Altman says that often agreements will be reached with acquired companies to stay fairly autonomous, which can be a great thing if you already like your work and its processes. "I would push the founders to make sure you get an agreement to operate as independently as possible," he advises.

Unfortunately, even if such an agreement is reached, the reality of what "staying independent" looks like can be vastly different in each scenario. There may be certain processes like vacation time or required internal systems that will bend toward the parent company's way of doing things. Be prepared for this outcome, but keep an open mind. They also might have better perks than you currently have.

6. **Determine whether the new reality aligns with what's important to you, and decide which things are nonnegotiable for you.** Analiese Brown recommends reading *What Color Is Your Parachute?*, a classic career discovery book, which can help you do the crucial work of discovering what's important and what ultimately will be most fulfilling to you in your career.

Upon initially deciding to join the company, you probably evaluated a number of factors that you'll now have to reevaluate. These include:

- Preferred geographic location
- Office environment you thrive in
- Essential company values

Brown reminds us that it is a human impulse to fear
change. Figure out what's important to you personally.
Are you unwilling to move to a new city? Will you
draw the line if the acquiring company doesn't value
inclusiveness?
Brown also says coming back to your own needs and
desires provides a framework to evaluate whether the
new reality of your acquired company will support and
fulfill these things (or not). This personal inquiry is a
good checkpoint at many points in your career, but it
is especially crucial when your company is experiencing
major change. Don't glide into a company you're not
excited about just because you neglected to look for a
new job post-acquisition.

7. **If you have equity, understand how it works.**
Understanding the impact to you as soon as you can
will equip you with information about whether there's
a choice to be made, or whether there's an obligation to
you around how that is paid out.

If you don't have equity, you may feel like the ship
has sailed, but some individuals who were involved in
the transition or contributed heavily to the company's
success in the recent past may now be in a position to be
rewarded in some other way. That can be discretionary,
but it's worth having the conversation. If in doubt,
consider hiring a lawyer or business advisor who
specializes in startup equity; you'll be glad you did.

You may be acquired by a parent company with a
bonus or Management by Objectives (MBO) culture,
and if you're in a key position, you can negotiate with

the parent company for a favorable compensation structure or bonus. If you're someone integral to the transition, whether or not equity is part of your current compensation package, you may have some leverage.

8. **Consider negotiating for a new role or a promotion.** Incredible, new, and unexpected opportunities can often surface out of an acquisition. It may not even be something you have to ask for; you may experience a restructure and be asked to take on a new role, perhaps travel more, or be based out of an office in a more desirable location.

Often larger companies acquiring smaller ones may have more well-articulated career paths, or they may look at the role you're doing in a new way. At smaller companies, you may be a Jack or Jill of all trades, but upon acquisition, you may find that in this new reality, your multifaceted role puts you a peg higher in an organizational chart.

You may also find that you are qualified to be in a higher-level role, and the acquiring company will likely have more funds or resources for learning and development. This may include attending conferences, workshops, or an internally created leadership development program. There also may be more structured rewards and incentive programs.

In the early post-deal stages, Brown reminds us that it may not be totally clear what new career paths will be available or who will be impacted and how. In an ideal scenario, managers are a good first line of contact to ask for information and discuss how you'll be impacted along the way. Hopefully, your manager will have the inside track or be able to point you toward the right resources so you can explore promotions or other opportunities. A learner's mindset is the best way to survive any uncertainty.

Final Thoughts

If you're facing an acquisition, adopt a growth mindset and find ways to become an active participant in the transition. Your goal is not to try to resist the change or preserve the status quo, but rather to understand what the new scenario will be and to determine if the new company "reality" aligns with your values and needs.

The acquisition of your startup can be an incredibly powerful catalyst for your career and personal development—don't forget to enjoy the ride.

CHAPTER FIFTEEN

LIFE AFTER YOUR STARTUP ROLE

Startup employees can and do transition into founders, investors, and mentors. As you shape your career, you may choose to join their ranks.

To Entrepreneur and Back

"How come they don't say serial employee?"[46]
Startup veteran Noah Kagan tweeted this, asking why we don't talk about serial employees the way we do about serial entrepreneurs. Many of us, after reading all about how to become empowered as startup employees, will consider becoming founders or entrepreneurs, or freelance consultants. And we then may go back to being employees.

On Being a Startup Employee versus Entrepreneur

Should you be a startup founder? Unfortunately, the prevailing belief is that the inevitable conclusion of every successful startup career is founding your own company. But is that route right for you?

In *The Start-Up of You*, authors Reid Hoffman and Ben Casnocha say that many of us drawn to the startup ecosystem would be wise to think critically about whether we want to be a founder or employee—because there can be a lot of pressure to be a founder when most of us would be happier as employees.

You were born an entrepreneur. This doesn't mean you were born to start companies. In fact, most people shouldn't start companies. The long odds of success, combined with the constant emotional whiplash, makes starting a business the right path for only some people.[47]

If you're inclined to start a company, by all means do it. But if you're happier with your current trajectory as a team member, don't let the myth that we should all become founders sway you from what feels right.

Transitioning from Founder to Employee and Back

Perhaps you're thinking about becoming a founder and wondering whether you can rejoin another startup afterward. Questions that often arise:

- If you become a founder, will you be able to transition back to employee?
- Are you then always branded a founder, or can you one day return to the world of being an employee?

We frequently talk about founders as if they are a unique category; one is an entrepreneur, and this quality defines them and their career. But the reality is that the categories *founder* and *employee* are not as fixed as we may believe. Many entrepreneurs choose to become employees after failures or exits from companies that were potentially successful but not home runs.

After selling his Boulder, Colorado-based startup Uvize, entrepreneur Dave Cass accepted a Senior Product Manager role at another technology startup. When he was no longer in the founder role, Cass grappled with the change in identity. "When I was transitioning (from entrepreneur to employee), that was a huge fear of mine. Will I not feel like an entrepreneur? There is pride in starting and ownership," says Cass.

Like Cass, many entrepreneurs with whom I've spoken have gone back to being employees after selling their companies. Tom Krackeler has made a career out of this; he builds companies and then joins them as an employee. Most recently, he is currently SVP of Product at Zuora after they acquired his company Frontleaf. Founders who have made the transition back to employee sometimes feel frustrated, but often they also feel that the stability of getting a full-time paycheck plus the mental freedom of not having it all on their shoulders provides advantages that outweigh this.

Being Your Own Boss: Freelance Consulting

Being a freelancer or consultant is becoming increasingly common—and enticing. The opportunity to set your own schedule, work with clients on your own terms, and (ideally) only work on things that truly interest you can be hard to resist. I, for one, couldn't.

I was a consultant for nearly five years, and it profoundly changed the trajectory of my career. It enabled me to focus on my "zone of genius" and work with many more startups than I would have as an employee. Now, as a director of marketing a decade into my career, while most of my peers have several tech startup company experiences under their belts, I have dozens.

The experience of consulting for so many companies within an industry gave me exposure to how different tech companies operate. It provided me with an understanding of the patterns and challenges B2B SaaS companies face in marketing. It taught me how to think like a business owner. If I didn't deliver results, I knew my clients wouldn't renew our monthly contracts, so I became relentlessly outcome-oriented. This isn't the right path for everyone. If you're thinking of consulting, consider starting with one or two clients on the side outside of your "day job" and see if you like it.

How to find freelancing opportunities:

- Join Upwork and start a freelancer profile.
- Ask your network if they're looking for consulting help.
- Browse Craigslist for contract work or respond to job postings for full-time (FT) roles and see if they need help in the interim while they're hiring for a FT role (this actually does work).
- Contact former employers and see if they would be open to contract work.

A few tips for being a tech company freelancer:

- **Be professional.** Get really good WiFi in your home office or get a coworking space. Ensure your work environment is as quiet as possible. Treat your freelancing business like the real business that it is.

- **Keep in touch with former clients.** You never know when they'll need help; maybe a former client will even start a new company and need your help.
- **Bill clients for outcomes, not your time.** It's OK if you charge per hour at first, but this isn't a winning strategy. As an employee, you weren't paid for the hours you spent at your desk; you were paid to drive results in your role. Research how you can create packages and solutions for your work versus selling hours.
- **Hire a lawyer to look over any confusing statements of work (SOWs).** Better yet, create your own SOW template and have it approved by a lawyer, then send it to clients when you're pitching work. Make sure you're not getting yourself into any sticky contractual situations.
- **Make friends with other freelancers.** Join a Slack community for freelancers, connect with a co-working community, attend happy hours and meetups for freelancers, and do what you can to build a virtual and online freelancer community. You can hire each other for projects, or at the very least, keep each other motivated when work piles up or dries up (both situations are challenging).
- **Take unplugged vacations.** Really. It can feel harder as a freelancer for many reasons—you're working for yourself, so any time you take off is money out of the bank account—but if you don't want to burn out, you have to do this.

- **Build up a personal reference network and success portfolio.** Clients will hire you much faster when they can easily see how others have benefitted from your work.

- **Get an accountant.** There are a lot of financial considerations you'll need to take into account when you're your own employer, and a good accountant will help you identify deductions, figure out which retirement accounts to use to maximize tax benefits, and more.

- **Keep building your personal brand.** As a freelancer, building your personal brand is even more important; this is what will help you continue to get gigs.

A few downsides to freelancing:

- Paying for your own medical insurance and not receiving PTO

- Spending time on admin for your business (marketing, accounting, etc.) that you'd otherwise be spending on the work itself if you were an employee

- Only getting paid when you work, making taking a vacation harder to justify

- Experiencing social isolation and loneliness if you are used to showing up at an office every day and don't have a good support network. This can also be true of remote work, but it's on a whole other level as a freelancer because there is no one group to center around. Join a Slack or in-person community to combat this.

More suggested resources:

- *Double Your Freelancing Rate* by Brennan Dunn
- Earn1K course by Ramit Sethi

In 2015 three of my self-funded B2B SaaS startup clients were acquired, and I had offers to join two of them. When I accepted an offer and returned to full-time employee status, it felt like a relief. I could work at a company I loved without the administrative overhead of being a freelancer. I was able to slide into the perfect role for me, with a great team, because I had already worked with them as a freelance consultant. Don't be afraid to let a consulting gig you love turn into a full-time role!

Be a Mentor and Advisor

Everyone is a mentor—including you.

In *Startup Communities*, VC Brad Feld describes the mentor-mentee relationship. He says, "The best moment in a mentor-mentee relationship is when the mentor learns as much, or more, from the mentee."[48]

As you grow your career, it can be incredibly fulfilling to find ways to give back; mentoring and advising can be as satisfying and gratifying for you as for those whom you mentor. You can mentor someone no matter where you are in your career. Think of those with less expertise, either within your company or even at a local school.

Entrepreneur Mandy Godown says:

You can be early on in your career and mentor someone further along; you could have a new insight into a technology or can provide advice on how to connect with your generation. When you're there for someone else and helping them navigate this complex world of work and life, there's a wealth of good that comes to the person offering that. It adds to our level of confidence. It can help us feel better to help someone else's life and career. And you never know the dividends it will pay down the line when they are able to help you too.

MergeLane Co-founder Sue Heilbronner says this about mentorship:

The word *mentor* has become generic; mentees should be extremely discerning about whom they select as mentors. The most important characteristic of a good mentor-mentee relationship is personal connection and chemistry. Once you get through facts like this person has great experience in finance and this person could use some bolstering in their knowledge, once you find that content expertise or knowledge gap expertise, connection is the most important thing.

Mentees are most successful when they think about identifying mentors as people who are already in their world with whom they have a big connection; it's true for mentors also. We have formal structure in accelerators, incubators, and that's all fantastic as a way to facilitate and enhance the power of mentorship, but informal opportunities can be very meaningful. It's true, I know more people looking for mentors than people looking for mentees, but the reason I think that's true is young people are told "go find mentors," and I don't think mid-career people are told to go find mentees.

Mentoring isn't for everyone. I really like when people contribute to community; everyone can do that in different ways. In our community of Boulder, substantial parts that keep it together are investors and sponsors. Some of those sponsors are also mentors. Some of them are not. No matter what, having sponsors to support programs that help startups get more visibility in the community is critical to our ecosystem. What's the zone of genius for you? If mentoring is a zone of genius, go be a mentor. If you have a wish to commit other resources, there are people in our community who voluntarily offer support for building financial models to help them visualize their business. It's mentorship, and it's also giving a zone of genius in a stage that makes meaningful sense.

Sponsorship versus Mentorship

A sponsor is willing to take a risk and bet on you. Marketing executive Rachel Beisel says:

I would be willing to risk my reputation to help the person throughout their career, which is more than a mentor, who maybe supports you but isn't willing to put their reputation on the line. A sponsor is vested in the future progression of someone. They know that that person they are sponsoring will make them look good and they will get something in return down the road as well. It's a two-way street. That person you sponsor encourages you to take risks and has your back. I've done this throughout my career. They also deliver critical feedback. A sponsor expects a great deal in return versus a mentor, who doesn't expect much, including performance, loyalty, and advice down the road.

Beisel says she is still in touch with the people she has sponsored many years later, and has continued to find ways to work with them throughout their career.

Startup entrepreneur Donnya Piggott says:

It's just as important to have a mentor as it is to be one. The majority of my insight comes from my advising other people; I always learn something and often can take my own advice. It's all about perspective. That can put you in a bubble. By stepping outside of it, that's important. And if you can help someone else do that, you can make a big impact. Sometimes the advice you have for others applies to yourself, and it's a great reminder.

You likely have skills or knowledge that can help someone at another stage or in another department. We can all be allies to each other and help others grow in the industry. A mentor can see you outside of yourself and give you perspective and insight that enables you to avoid mistakes (or at least make different ones).

You don't have to be an expert in a field to be a mentor; you just have to be able to understand a person's vision, who they are, and what they need to do to get there. Mentorship, including at the peer level, is a lesser-discussed but incredibly important currency of our startup world. If you don't feel you can offer knowledge, you can at least offer encouragement and emotional support. After all, startup life can be hard and exhausting. It is important to also be mindful of your own time and energy and avoid overextending yourself in the process of helping others. That being said, if you have some bandwidth, mentoring is one of the most fulfilling aspects of startup life!

AFTERWORD

At the beginning of this book, I introduced you to a group of friends sitting around discussing our startup careers. It is my hope that this book can act as a version of that gathering. The startup world can be a tough, lonely place. It can also be a source of hope, inspiration, and empowerment. Together we have the power to shape the startup industry. I sincerely hope that this book has helped you in some way—at the very least to know you are not alone in your journey. As you venture forth, intrepid startup person, it is my wish that you believe in yourself and your ability to shape the tech industry with your talents. No matter your background, you have something to contribute. If you want to be in the startup world, you belong here.

If you liked the book, please encourage others to grab a copy, and leave a review online to help spread the word. Here's to your startup journey!

In power,
Sarah

ACKNOWLEDGMENTS

Thank you first of all to my brother, Asher Brown, who has enthusiastically supported both me and this project from infancy. Brother, you are truly the best. Thank you to my parents, Mark and Joan Brown, and grandmother, Zelda Lipman, for providing love and support. It means the world! I am grateful to Samuel Hulick and Eliot Peper, both of whom have provided indispensable feedback, advice, and motivation countless times throughout the journey of writing and publishing this book. Thank you to Hiten Shah and Steli Efti, who took breaks from podcasting with each other and running their companies to share their ideas and support. (Hiten: Our eight-minute phone calls were true lifesavers.) Thank you to Brad Feld and Jeffrey Bussgang for providing invaluable guidance and support. Thank you to the wise and extraordinarily kind Lodi Siefer for reminding me that when navigating uncertain territory, the map is always inside of us. I am grateful to Paul Lambert for his generous and insightful feedback. Thank you to Nicolle Paradise, who generously pored over the manuscript and provided instrumental feedback. Thank you to Rachel and Lupe Fuchs for our many supportive, meaningful, and joyful walks around Boulder in between writing sessions. Thank you to Hannah Davis, Marshall Hayes, Aaron Davis, Katie Breen,

Worth Baker, and Julie Penner for being sounding boards and north stars and for providing key guidance and support at every step of the project. Thank you to Colleen Blake, Daniel Luebke, Erin Rand, Samyukta Sankaran, Mary Carter, Rob Castaneda, Rodrigo Luna, Bill Cushard, and many other Rocketeers for teaching me so much about startups and life, and for sharing many of the principles and insights that made it into this book.

Thank you to Dustin DeVan, Jesse Pedersen, and David Malpass for convincing me to join your outstanding team and for helping me stretch and grow as a leader in the process. Thank you to Martha Knauf for her savvy copyediting and vital feedback. I am grateful to Matt Harada, who provided motivational support and instrumental constructive criticism that made this book markedly better. Thank you to those who provided support and key feedback along the way, including Joel Spolsky, Allen Chong, Jaime Roth, Rachel Zurer, Rylee Keys, Carly Gloge, Danny Kramer, Adena Kling, Aubrey Blanche, Anima Singh, Shira Frank, Matt Hessler, Lisa Brownstone, Jo Caldwell, Chris Senesi, Tamara Hale, Nick Verbeck, Josie Martinez, Scott Yates, Acacia O'Connor, Dennis Adsit, Sue Heilbronner, Kimberly Kosmenko, Jim Franklin, Kate Catlin, Mischa Delaney, Gerry Valentine, Alana Moskowitz, Jo and Kim Fleming, Courtney Petrie, and Mandy Godown. Thank you to the contributors who shared stories that made it into the book, including: Matt Harada, Matt Hessler, Hiten Shah, Brad Feld, Dave Cass, Josh Ashton, Andrew Hyde, Sarah Innocenzi, Sandijs Ruluks, Natalie Baumgartner, Mandy Godown, Carly Brantz, Yoav Lurie, Donnya Piggott, Peter Bell, Analiese Brown, and

Rachel Beisel. Thank you to my wonderful writing coach and editor Anne Janzer who provided crucial input and support every step of the way. This book has benefited from the editors, designers, and coaches with whom I have worked, including Karen Strauss, Ayse Yilmaz, Claudia Volkman, Debra Orenstein, Emma Hall, and Kevin Kane.

I am also indebted to every startup team with whom I have ever worked, and to everyone who has shared thoughts, stories, and feedback about this project, including those whose stories aren't included in these pages. To those I haven't named here, but who have provided feedback along the way, I owe you my sincerest gratitude for your contributions and support. This book would not exist without you.

NOTES

1. Note: Names have been changed.
2. "Why Startups Fail, According to Their Founders," Fortune. com, September 25, 2014, http://fortune.com/2014/09/25/why-startups-fail-according-to-their-founders/.
3. https://www.amazon.com/Start-up-You-Future-Yourself-Transform-ebook/dp/B0050DIWHU.
4. Moritz Plassnig, "Hiring, the Single Most Important Skill as a Founder," http://www.techstars.com/content/accelerators/boston/hiring-the-single-most-important-skill-as-a-founder/.
5. Jenny Lefcourt, "Beware of the Beautiful Resume," https://smallbusinessforum.co/beware-of-the-beautiful-resume-60bed7f8bba0#.y25ch430d.
6. Clayton M. Christensen, *The Innovator's Dilemma: When New Technologies Cause Great Firms to Fail* (Boston: Harvard Business Review Press, 2016).
7. Patrick McGeehan, "Half of New York's Tech Workers Lack College Degrees, Report Says," *New York Times*, April 1, 2014, https://www.nytimes.com/2014/04/02/nyregion/half-of-new-yorks-tech-workers-lack-college-degrees-report-says.html?ref=technology&_r=1.
8. "How to Get a Job at a Startup," episode 110, The Startup Chat, https://thestartupchat.com/ep110/
9. Sheryl O'Loughlin, *Killing It: An Entrepreneur's Guide to Keeping Your Head Without Losing Your Heart* (New York: Harper Business, 2016), p. 5.
10. "Transparent Funding Announcements," Feld Thoughts, http://www.feld.com/archives/2015/04/

bringing-depression-shadows-startups.html.

11. Aimee Groth, "Startups Are Now Pitching Mental Wellness Like a Perk," Quartz.com, December 15, 2016, https://qz.com/854828/startups-are-now-pitching-mental-wellness-like-a-perk/

12. Katie Benner, "Silicon Valley Dream Collapses in Allegations of Fraud," August 31, 2016, https://www.nytimes.com/2016/09/01/technology/a-silicon-valley-dream-collapses-in-allegations-of-fraud.htmls.

13. The Startup Chat with Steli and Hiten, https://itunes.apple.com/us/podcast/startup-chat-steli-hiten/id997616345?mt=2.

14. Deborah Gage, "The Venture Capital Secret: 3 out of 4 Start-Ups Fail," *Wall Street Journal*, Sept. 20, 2012.

15. https://en.wikipedia.org/wiki/Unicorn_(finance).

16. Jeffrey Bussgang, *Entering StartUpLand: An Essential Guide to Finding the Right Job* (Boston: Harvard Business Review Press, 2017), p. 10.

17. Financial Samurai, "Candid Advice for Those Joining The Startup World: Sleep with One Eye Open," http://www.financialsamurai.com/candid-advice-for-those-joining-the-startup-world/#sthash.sDzEb8uM.dpuf.

18. Sally Bolig, "Risk vs Reward—How to Choose a Startup," CloserIQ, http://blog.closeriq.com/2016/12/choosing-a-startup/?utm_campaign=Mattermark+Daily&utm_source=hs_email&utm_medium=email&utm_content=39598406&_hsenc=p2ANqtz--NLJ0tIvG6glRysCdpaEIyFoHhN1eVMIcj7N8CE9M6M8rgZu0KytMhhduH34DR6r1akzZ7HDavnzKVjP_sWLZfNnITjHRNlGSxJzKN5pJ4jU10EY&_hsmi=39598406.

19. Eric Weiner, *The Geography of Genius: Lessons from the World's Most Creative Places* (New York: Simon & Schuster, 2016).

20. Robert H. Frank, "What Price the High Moral Ground?" Cornell University; http://www.people.vcu. edu/~lrazzolini/GR1997.pdf.

21. Robert H. Frank, "The Incalculable Value of Finding a Job You Love," *New York Times*, July 22, 2016.

22. Jenna Wortham, "The New Dream Jobs," *New York Times Magazine*, February 28, 2016.

23. https://www.slideshare.net/reed2001/culture-1798664/7-Actual_company_values_are_thebehaviors.

24. "Netflix Culture," Netflix Jobs, https://jobs.netflix.com/culture.

25. Avram Joel Spolsky, *Smart & Gets Things Done* (Apress, 2007).

26. Building Connected, https://www.buildingconnected.com/jobs/.

27. "Women in Tech: The Facts" (2016 Update), National Center for Women & Information Technology, https://www.ncwit.org/resources/women-tech-facts-2016-update.

28. Analiese Brown, "What Your Company's Dirty Dishes Can Tell You About Your Team's Engagement Level," Medium, https://medium.com/@analiesebrown/what-your-companys-dishwasher-can-tell-you-about-your-team-s-engagement-level-fe38d677605b.

29. Jess Ryan, "5 Roles That Prove You Don't Need to Code to Work for a Startup," Built in Colorado, http://www.builtincolorado.com/2016/10/13/how-to-work-in-tech-without-coding-skills?utm_content=buffer-

POWER TO THE STARTUP PEOPLE

ab90c&utm_medium=social&utm_source=linkedin.
com&utm_campaign=buffer.

30. Carol S. Dweck, *Mindset: The New Psychology of Success*
(New York: Random House, 2006), pp. 68, 125, 142.

31. Brian Balfour, "7 Things I Wish I Knew When I Started
My Career," Buffer, https://stories.buffer.com/7-things-i-
wish-i-knew-when-i-started-my-career-c69be5d55d54.

32. Ibid.

33. Whitney Johnson, *Disrupt Yourself: Putting the Power of
Disruptive Innovation to Work* (New York: Routledge, 2016),
p. 25.

34. Adi Gaskell, "Why a Flexible Worker Is a Happy and
Productive Worker," Forbes.com; https://www.forbes.com/
sites/adigaskell/2016/01/15/why-a-flexible-worker-is-a-hap-
py-and-productive-worker/#7bdf348314c4.

35. *Killing It*, p. 129.

36. Colleen Blake, "Advice for Female Leaders on Career
Acceleration, Setting Work Boundaries and Accepting
Help," Sharp Heels.com; http://sharpheels.com/2016/06/
juggling-work-home/.

37. Josh Pigford, "How We're Fixing Unlimited
Vacation," Baremetrics, https://baremetrics.com/blog/
unlimited-minimum-vacation.

38. Ylan Q. Mui, "Study: Women with More Children Are
More Productive at Work," WashingtonPost.com ;
https://www.washingtonpost.com/news/wonk/
wp/2014/10/30/study-women-with-more-children-are-
more-productive-at-work/?noredirect=on&utm_term=.
d7c3c6f47def.

39. *Killing It*, p.133.

40. Chris Holt, "You Know It's Time to Leave Your Startup When . . ."; TheBoldItalic.com; https://thebolditalic.com/you-know-it-s-time-to-leave-your-start-up-when-the-bold-italic-san-francisco-fbae5575e4e8.

41. Cameron Keng, "Employees Who Stay in Companies Longer Than Two Years Get Paid 50% Less," Forbes.com; https://www.forbes.com/sites/cameronkeng/2014/06/22/employees-that-stay-in-companies-longer-than-2-years-get-paid-50-less/#70dab8c8e07f.

42. Matt Simon, "Restricted Stock Units: The Essential Facts," https://www.schwab.com/public/eac/resources/articles/rsu_facts.html.

43. G. Richard Shell, *Bargaining for Advantage: Negotiation Strategies for Reasonable People* (New York: Penguin, 2006).

44. Reid Hoffman and Ben Casnocha, *The Start-Up of You:Adapt to the Future, Invest in Yourself, and Transform Your Career* (New York: Currency, 2012)

45. Office Hours with Sam Altman, Y Combinator, https://blog.ycombinator.com/office-hours-with-sam-altman/?utm_campaign=Mattermark+Daily&utm_source=hs_email&utm_medium=email&utm_content=40587476&_hsenc=p2ANqtz-8kGGQRYxtUwGrxqnesw06aWLZwmBE-HCc-CSSe98CyxtTz6awxitEogeIYyGjWuNO9FrBOJwt-FVut1zWRZEgpdMYunevsZIOSZg2Svxc5dKQlAbptBI&_hsmi=40587476%22.

46. https://twitter.com/noahkaganstatus/70349827938484221

47. *The Start-Up of You*, p. 1.

48. Brad Feld, *Startup Communities: Building an Entrepreneurial Ecosystem in Your City* (Hoboken, New Jersey: Wiley, 2012).

RECOMMENDED READING

If you're interested in learning more about startups and start-up life, here are some additional recommended books to check out.

Bargaining for Advantage: Negotiation Strategies for Reasonable People, G. Richard Shell

Brotopia: Breaking Up the Boys' Club of Silicon Valley, Emily Chang

Built for Growth: How Builder Personality Shapes Your Business, Your Team, and Your Ability to Win, Chris Kuenne and John Danner

Bullshit Jobs: A Theory, David Graeber

Business Without the Bullsh*t, Geoffrey James

Chaos Monkeys: Obscene Fortune and Random Failure in Silicon Valley, Antonio García Martínez

Close to the Machine: Technophilia and Its Discontents, Ellen Ullman

Crossing the Chasm: Marketing and Selling Disruptive Products to Mainstream Customers, Geoffrey A. Moore

Customer Success: How Innovative Companies Are Reducing Churn and Growing Recurring Revenue, Nick Mehta, Dan Steinman, and Lincoln Murphy

Do More Faster: TechStars Lessons to Accelerate Your Startup, Brad Feld and David Cohen

Entering StartUpLand, Jeffrey Bussgang

Getting to Yes: Negotiating Agreement Without Giving In, Roger Fisher, William L. Ury, and Bruce Patton

Good to Great: Why Some Companies Make the Leap . . . and Others Don't, Jim Collins

High Growth Handbook, Elad Gil

Killing It, Sheryl O'Loughlin

Lean In: Women, Work, and the Will to Lead, Sheryl Sandberg

Lost and Founder: A Painfully Honest Field Guide to the Startup World, Rand Fishkin

Made to Stick: Why Some Ideas Survive and Others Die, Chip Heath and Dan Heath

Mindset: The New Psychology of Success, Carol Dweck

Minority Leader: How to Lead from the Outside and Make Real Change, Stacey Abrams

Option B: Facing Adversity, Building Resilience, And Finding Joy, Sheryl Sandberg

Powerful: Building a Culture of Freedom and Responsibility, Patty McCord

Principles: Life and Work, Ray Dalio

Radical Candor: Be a Kick-Ass Boss Without Losing Your Humanity, Kim Scott

Remote: Office Not Required, Jason Fried

Smart and Gets Things Done: Joel Spolsky's Concise Guide to Finding the Best Technical Talent, Avram Joel Spolsky

Startup Life: Surviving and Thriving in a Relationship, Brad Feld and Amy Batchelor

Startup Opportunities: Know When to Quit Your Day Job, Sean Wise and Brad Feld

Start with Why: How Great Leaders Inspire Everyone to Take Action, Simon Sinek

Subscription Marketing: Strategies for Nurturing Customers in a World of Churn, Ann Janzer

The Hard Thing About Hard Things: Building a Business When There Are No Easy Answers, Ben Horowitz

The Idea Factory: Bell Labs and the Great Age of American Innovation, John Gertner

The Innovator's Dilemma: When New Technologies Cause Great Firms to Fail, Clayton Christensen

The Lean Startup: How Today's Entrepreneurs Use Continuous Innovation to Create Radically Successful Businesses, Eric Ries

The Start-Up of You: Adapt to the Future, Invest in Yourself, and Transform Your Career, Reid Hoffman and Ben Casnocha

Traction: Get a Grip on Your Business, Gino Wickman

Troublemakers: Silicon Valley's Coming of Age, Leslie Berlin

Index

A

Accenture 35
acquisition vi, 133, 134, 135, 140, 141, 142, 144, 145, 146
acquisitions 139, 140
ADP 19
agenda 75, 79
Allen, David 69, 160
Altman, Sam 142, 167
Amplio Digital 19, 110
Annual Recurring Revenue (ARR) 21
Ashton, Josh 111, 112, 113, 115, 116, 117
Atlassian Jira 72
Austin, Texas 27
Australia 97

B

Backstage Capital 42
Balfour, Brian 73, 166
BareMetrics 96
Bargaining for Advantage 110, 118, 167, 169
Batchelor, Amy 13, 171
Baumgartner, Natalie 38
bias 5, 45, 55
biases 45
BlackBirds 44
Blackforce 44
Blake, Colleen 93, 160, 166
bootcamp 126, 127, 128, 129

R

S

T

About the Author

Sarah E. Brown is a B2B tech marketing leader, founder of Flatirons Tech, a diversity- and inclusion-focused tech meetup based in Boulder, Colorado, and mentor to early-stage startups at Techstars accelerator. Sarah frequently contributes to industry blogs and publications and speaks about marketing, customer success, increasing startup inclusivity, and growing your startup career. She blogs at http://www. sarahbrownmarketing.com, and you can find her on Twitter @SEBMarketing. A Boulderite for many years, Sarah now lives in the San Francisco Bay Area, where she enjoys being immersed in the tech startup capital of the world, hiking, sailing, and drinking robot-made vegan cappuccinos.

www.ingramcontent.com/pod-product-compliance
Lightning Source LLC
Chambersburg PA
CBHW071605210326
41597CB00019B/3411